BUILDING CHATBOTS WITH PYTHON

Create Smart and Interactive Bots
with Natural Language Processing

THOMPSON CARTER

TABLE OF CONTENTS

Introduction

Building Chatbots with Python: Create Smart and Interactive Bots with Natural Language Processing

In recent years, chatbots have become an integral part of how businesses, services, and individuals interact with technology. Whether you're booking a flight, getting weather updates, or asking for technical support, chatbots have revolutionized how we access information and services. The core of this transformation lies in the ability of chatbots to understand human language and respond intelligently, thanks to advances in **Natural Language Processing (NLP)** and **Artificial Intelligence (AI)**.

This book, *Building Chatbots with Python: Create Smart and Interactive Bots with Natural Language Processing*, is designed to be a comprehensive guide for anyone interested in developing chatbots using Python. With the increasing demand for conversational interfaces across industries—from customer service and healthcare to e-commerce and entertainment—there has never been a better time to dive into this exciting field.

The goal of this book is to provide you with the knowledge, tools, and techniques required to build a chatbot from scratch, taking advantage of Python's rich ecosystem of libraries and frameworks. Whether you are a beginner to chatbot development or looking to deepen your understanding of NLP and AI, this book will guide you through the entire process, step by step.

Why Chatbots?

The growing use of chatbots in various sectors has led to a significant change in how we interact with computers. Unlike traditional applications, which require specific user actions, chatbots allow users to interact with technology in a more natural, conversational way. This shift not only enhances user experience but also reduces the barriers to accessing information and services.

Some of the reasons why chatbots have become so popular include:

- **24/7 Availability**: Chatbots never need to sleep, making them an invaluable tool for businesses that require constant availability.
- **Improved Customer Experience**: By providing instant responses and solutions to customer queries, chatbots can enhance customer satisfaction.
- **Cost Efficiency**: Chatbots can automate repetitive tasks, reducing the need for human agents and saving businesses time and money.
- **Personalization**: With the ability to track user preferences and behaviors, chatbots can offer a highly personalized experience, making interactions more engaging and relevant.

What This Book Will Teach You

In this book, we will explore the **fundamentals of chatbot development** and introduce you to the **power of Python** for building chatbots that are not only functional but also intelligent. You will learn how to implement sophisticated NLP techniques to enable your chatbot to understand user intent, process natural language, and interact in a meaningful way.

Here's what you will learn as you progress through this book:

1. **Getting Started with Chatbots and Python**: You'll begin by understanding what chatbots are, the different types of chatbots, and how Python is the ideal language for building intelligent chatbots. We'll set up your development environment and introduce you to essential libraries like **spaCy**, **NLTK**, and **TensorFlow**.

2. **Understanding NLP and AI Techniques**: You will explore key concepts in **Natural Language Processing (NLP)**, such as tokenization, stemming, lemmatization, and Named Entity Recognition (NER). We will dive into the power of **machine learning algorithms** for enhancing chatbot intelligence.

3. **Building Rule-Based Chatbots**: You will learn how to build a **rule-based chatbot** that uses predefined patterns to generate responses. This foundational approach will help you understand how more advanced models work.

4. **Developing Machine Learning-Based Chatbots**: As we move forward, we will introduce **machine learning models** for intent recognition, allowing your chatbot to better understand user queries. You will learn how to train, evaluate, and deploy these models effectively.

5. **Integrating Deep Learning Models**: We will explore the use of **deep learning** techniques such as **sequence-to-sequence models** and **transformers** for creating highly sophisticated chatbots. By the end of this section, you will be able to build chatbots capable of understanding context and maintaining engaging multi-turn conversations.

6. **Creating Multimodal and Voice-Enabled Chatbots**: You will expand your chatbot's capabilities by incorporating **speech recognition** for voice-based interactions, and learn how to integrate multimodal inputs such as images and video.

7. **Deploying Your Chatbot**: Finally, we'll guide you through the process of **deploying your chatbot** to the cloud, making it accessible to users through web and mobile interfaces. You will also learn best practices for ensuring the scalability, security, and performance of your chatbot.

8. **Enhancing User Experience (UX)**: A chatbot's success depends on its ability to engage and assist users. You will explore **user experience (UX)** design principles specifically tailored to chatbots, ensuring that your bot provides a seamless, intuitive, and personalized experience.

9. **Ensuring Security and Privacy**: As your chatbot may handle sensitive data, this book covers the importance of **data privacy** and **security** measures to protect users and comply with legal requirements, such as GDPR.

10. **The Future of Chatbots and NLP**: Finally, we will discuss emerging trends in chatbot technology, the growing role of **AI** and **NLP**, and the potential for future chatbot innovations, including advancements in conversational AI and multimodal experiences.

Who Should Read This Book?

This book is ideal for anyone interested in building intelligent chatbots using Python, whether you are:

- A **beginner** looking to understand the basics of chatbot development and NLP.
- An **experienced developer** seeking to enhance your chatbot's capabilities using machine learning and deep learning techniques.
- A **data scientist** or **AI enthusiast** interested in applying NLP and AI to real-world applications.
- A **business owner** or **entrepreneur** who wants to understand how chatbots can improve customer engagement and automate tasks.

Why Python?

Python is the most popular programming language for building chatbots, and for good reason. Python's **simplicity, rich ecosystem of libraries**, and **extensive community support** make it an ideal choice for chatbot development. Libraries like **spaCy, NLTK**, and **TensorFlow** provide powerful tools for processing natural language and building machine learning models, while frameworks like **Rasa** and **Flask** allow you to easily deploy your chatbot.

What You Need to Know

While this book is designed to be beginner-friendly, some familiarity with **Python programming** will help you get the most out of it. No prior knowledge of chatbot development or NLP is required. Each chapter provides clear, actionable steps to guide you through the process of building a chatbot, and you will be introduced to the key concepts and technologies as you progress.

Final Thoughts

As chatbots continue to shape the future of human-computer interaction, the demand for skilled chatbot developers will only grow. By the end of this book, you will have the skills to design, build, and deploy a wide range of chatbots—whether they are rule-based, machine learning-powered, or voice-enabled. You will also gain a solid understanding of NLP techniques and AI models, and how they can be applied to create smarter, more engaging chatbots.

With the knowledge and hands-on experience provided in this book, you'll be ready to tackle chatbot development with confidence, creating innovative solutions that meet the needs of users and businesses alike.

Chapter 1: Introduction to Chatbots

What Are Chatbots?

Chatbots are artificial intelligence (AI) systems that simulate human conversation through text or voice interactions. Their primary purpose is to automate communication and provide immediate responses to users' questions or requests. The term "chatbot" is derived from "chat" (as in conversation) and "bot" (short for robot), and they can operate on various platforms, including websites, messaging apps, or voice-based systems.

Chatbots work by processing user input, typically in the form of text or speech, and then returning a relevant response. The complexity of a chatbot depends on its underlying technology, which ranges from simple rule-based systems to more advanced AI-powered solutions.

Types of Chatbots: Rule-based vs. AI-based

1. **Rule-based Chatbots:**
   - **How They Work:** Rule-based chatbots operate based on predefined rules set by the developer. These rules define how the chatbot responds to specific user inputs. They rely on patterns and keywords to direct the flow of conversation.
   - **Strengths:**
     - Simplicity: Easy to build and maintain.

- Speed: Immediate responses for well-defined tasks.
- Cost-effective: Ideal for small businesses or tasks with limited complexity.

o **Limitations:**

- Limited to scripted responses and can only respond to known queries.
- Cannot handle ambiguous or unexpected questions effectively.

Example: A simple chatbot on an e-commerce website might ask users for their product preferences and provide a list of relevant items based on fixed keywords.

2. **AI-based Chatbots (Conversational AI):**

o **How They Work:** AI-based chatbots leverage natural language processing (NLP) and machine learning (ML) to understand and generate responses. These bots use algorithms to interpret user input, learn from previous interactions, and provide more dynamic, context-aware responses.

o **Strengths:**

- Can handle complex conversations and understand user intent.
- Learn and improve over time through machine learning models.

- Can handle diverse and unstructured inputs, providing a more natural conversational flow.
  - **Limitations:**
    - More complex to build and require more computational resources.
    - May take longer to train, and responses may not always be perfect, especially in early stages.

Example: A customer service chatbot using AI can understand a wide range of questions and offer responses based on the context, even if the question is phrased differently than expected.

Real-world Applications of Chatbots

Chatbots are revolutionizing the way businesses interact with customers, making processes more efficient and accessible. Here are some key real-world applications:

1. **Customer Support:**
   - Chatbots can automate responses to common inquiries, reducing wait times and enhancing customer satisfaction. They can be integrated into websites, messaging apps, or voice assistants to handle support tickets, order inquiries, and troubleshooting.

- o **Example:** A telecom company uses a chatbot to troubleshoot common network issues and guide users through basic setup steps.

2. **E-commerce and Retail:**
   - o Chatbots assist users in making purchases by recommending products, providing information on sales, and processing orders. They can also answer product-related questions, provide personalized offers, and guide users through the checkout process.
   - o **Example:** A fashion retailer uses a chatbot to suggest clothing based on users' preferences, helping customers find items they may like.

3. **Healthcare:**
   - o Chatbots are being used for appointment scheduling, symptom checking, and providing medical information. They can reduce the burden on healthcare professionals by addressing routine questions and assisting patients with basic health queries.
   - o **Example:** A health chatbot helps patients book appointments with doctors, provides medication reminders, and offers basic medical advice.

4. **Banking and Finance:**
   - o Chatbots in banking assist with checking account balances, making transactions, answering FAQs, and

providing financial advice. They enable customers to manage their finances quickly and easily without needing human intervention.

- o **Example:** A banking chatbot can help users transfer funds, check balances, and report lost cards, all via a messaging interface.

5. **Education:**

- o Educational chatbots serve as tutors, answering student questions, providing learning resources, and even assisting with administrative tasks like course registration and exam scheduling.

- o **Example:** A chatbot in an online learning platform helps students with their coursework by answering academic queries and offering personalized study materials.

6. **Travel and Hospitality:**

- o Chatbots in the travel industry can assist with flight bookings, hotel reservations, and providing recommendations for destinations and activities.

- o **Example:** A chatbot helps travelers book flights, recommend hotels, and provide real-time updates about flight status.

7. **Entertainment and Media:**

- o Chatbots are used to enhance user engagement by recommending movies, TV shows, or music based on user preferences.
- o **Example:** A streaming service uses a chatbot to recommend movies based on a user's past viewing history.

As chatbots continue to evolve, their scope of applications is expanding, and they are expected to play an even larger role in automating tasks across industries. Their ability to handle routine tasks allows human workers to focus on more complex issues, making businesses more efficient while enhancing customer experience.

Chapter 2: Python Basics for Building Chatbots

Setting up Python Environment

Before you begin building chatbots, it's important to set up a Python environment that ensures all your tools and dependencies work smoothly. Here's how you can get started:

1. **Installing Python:**
    -   **Download Python:** Go to the official Python website and download the latest version of Python. Ensure that you select the option to "Add Python to PATH" during installation.
    -   **Verify Installation:** Open the command line or terminal and type:

        bash

        python --version

        This command will confirm that Python is installed and show you the installed version.

2. **Setting Up a Virtual Environment:** Virtual environments allow you to isolate your project's dependencies, making sure that your chatbot project won't interfere with other Python projects.

o **Create a Virtual Environment:** In your project folder, run:

bash

python -m venv mychatbotenv

Replace mychatbotenv with the name you want for your virtual environment.

o **Activate the Virtual Environment:**

- On Windows:

    bash

    mychatbotenv\Scripts\activate

- On macOS/Linux:

    bash

    source mychatbotenv/bin/activate

o **Install Required Packages:** After activating the virtual environment, you can install necessary libraries using pip (Python's package installer). For example, to install nltk (Natural Language Toolkit), you can use:

```
bash
```

```
pip install nltk
```

- o **Deactivating the Virtual Environment:** Once you're done, deactivate the virtual environment by typing:

```
bash
```

```
deactivate
```

3. **Setting Up an IDE (Integrated Development Environment):** A good IDE can help you write and manage your chatbot code more effectively. Popular choices include:
   - o **Visual Studio Code (VS Code):** Lightweight, with extensive plugin support for Python.
   - o **PyCharm:** A powerful Python-specific IDE, ideal for larger projects.
   - o **Jupyter Notebook:** If you prefer working in an interactive environment, especially for experimenting with code.

Key Python Libraries for Chatbot Development

To build a chatbot, you'll need various Python libraries that simplify the process of handling natural language, managing user input, and integrating machine learning models. Here are some essential libraries:

1. **NLTK (Natural Language Toolkit):**

   o **Purpose:** NLTK is one of the most popular libraries for working with human language data in Python. It provides tools for text processing, including tokenization, stemming, and part-of-speech tagging.

   o **Installation:**

   bash

   ```
   pip install nltk
   ```

   o **Use Case:** NLTK is great for tasks like text preprocessing, such as breaking sentences into words (tokenization) or identifying word stems.

2. **SpaCy:**

   o **Purpose:** SpaCy is a powerful and efficient library for advanced NLP tasks like named entity recognition (NER), part-of-speech tagging, and dependency parsing.

   o **Installation:**

   bash

   ```
   pip install spacy
   ```

   o **Use Case:** SpaCy is preferred for larger-scale NLP tasks and works well with deep learning-based models.

3. **TensorFlow and Keras (for Machine Learning Models):**

   o **Purpose:** TensorFlow is an open-source library for machine learning, and Keras is an easy-to-use wrapper for TensorFlow, enabling rapid prototyping of deep learning models.

   o **Installation:**

   bash

   pip install tensorflow

   o **Use Case:** These libraries are used for building and training machine learning models, such as neural networks for intent classification or response generation.

4. **ChatterBot:**

   o **Purpose:** ChatterBot is a Python library designed specifically for building conversational chatbots. It allows you to train your chatbot on different datasets and improve its responses through machine learning.

   o **Installation:**

   bash

   pip install chatterbot

o **Use Case:** ChatterBot is useful for beginners who want a simple, rule-based chatbot that improves over time based on interaction data.

5. **Flask (for Web Integration):**

   o **Purpose:** Flask is a lightweight Python web framework that allows you to create web applications. It can be used to deploy your chatbot on a website or integrate it into web-based platforms.

   o **Installation:**

   bash

   pip install flask

   o **Use Case:** Flask can be used to deploy a chatbot built with Python on a server so that it is accessible through a web interface.

6. **SpeechRecognition (for Voice-based Chatbots):**

   o **Purpose:** This library allows you to add speech recognition capabilities to your chatbot, enabling users to interact with the chatbot using voice commands.

   o **Installation:**

   bash

   pip install SpeechRecognition

- ○ **Use Case:** If you're building a voice chatbot, this library will convert audio input into text, which can then be processed by the chatbot.

Introduction to Basic Python Concepts Needed for Chatbot Development

For chatbot development, you'll need a basic understanding of Python fundamentals. Here are the key concepts you should know:

1. **Variables and Data Types:**
   - ○ Python supports several data types, including strings, integers, floats, booleans, and lists. These are essential when handling user input and storing chatbot responses.
   - ○ **Example:**

     python

     ```
     user_name = "Alice"
     user_age = 30
     user_input = "Hello, how are you?"
     ```

2. **Control Flow (Conditionals and Loops):**
   - ○ Control flow statements (like if, else, and elif) allow you to make decisions based on user input.

o Loops (for, while) are used to repeat actions, which is helpful when you need the chatbot to keep interacting until a certain condition is met.

o **Example:**

python

```
if user_input == "Hello":
    response = "Hi there!"
elif user_input == "Goodbye":
    response = "See you later!"
else:
    response = "I'm sorry, I didn't understand that."
```

3. **Functions:**

o Functions help you break down complex chatbot behavior into manageable chunks of code. They make the chatbot's code modular and easier to maintain.

o **Example:**

python

```
def greet_user(name):
    return f"Hello, {name}!"

user_name = "Alice"
greeting = greet_user(user_name)
print(greeting)
```

4. **Handling Strings:**

   o   Chatbot interactions often involve processing and manipulating strings, such as extracting keywords or performing case-insensitive comparisons.

   o   **Example:**

   python

   ```python
   message = "Hello, How can I help you today?"
   lower_message = message.lower()  # Convert to lowercase for uniformity
   ```

5. **Lists and Dictionaries:**

   o   Lists and dictionaries are essential data structures for storing multiple items, such as user queries or predefined chatbot responses.

   o   **Example:**

   python

   ```python
   responses = {
       "hello": "Hi! How can I assist you?",
       "bye": "Goodbye! Have a great day!"
   }
   user_input = "hello"
   print(responses.get(user_input, "Sorry, I didn't understand that."))
   ```

6. **Libraries and Importing Modules:**

o   Python allows you to import pre-written code from libraries and modules to extend your chatbot's capabilities. Familiarity with importing and using libraries is essential.

o   **Example:**

python

```
import nltk
from nltk.tokenize import word_tokenize
```

With these basic Python concepts and libraries, you're well on your way to building a chatbot. The next chapters will dive deeper into NLP and more advanced techniques, but mastering these fundamentals is key to developing a functional and interactive bot.

Chapter 3: Overview of Natural Language Processing (NLP)

What is NLP and Why Is It Essential for Chatbots?

Natural Language Processing (NLP) is a subfield of artificial intelligence (AI) that focuses on the interaction between computers and human (natural) languages. The goal of NLP is to enable machines to read, understand, interpret, and generate human language in a way that is both meaningful and useful. In the context of chatbots, NLP is essential because it allows the bot to interpret and respond to user input in a natural, human-like manner.

Without NLP, a chatbot would simply follow predefined scripts, making it limited to specific responses. With NLP, chatbots can understand the context of the conversation, identify user intentions, and generate more dynamic and relevant responses. This makes the interaction more fluid and user-friendly, much like speaking to a human representative.

Why NLP is Crucial for Chatbots:

- **Understanding User Intent:** NLP helps the chatbot understand the user's intent, even when the query is phrased in various ways.

- **Context Management:** NLP enables chatbots to manage ongoing conversations and retain context across multiple turns of dialogue.

- **Handling Variations in Language:** NLP allows chatbots to handle synonyms, slang, and grammatical differences in how users communicate, making the bot more flexible and adaptable.

- **Natural Interactions:** NLP makes chatbots capable of generating human-like, conversational responses that improve the user experience.

Key NLP Techniques

1. **Tokenization:**
   - **What It Is:** Tokenization is the process of breaking down text into smaller units, called tokens (which could be words, phrases, or characters).
   - **Why It Matters:** Tokenization allows the chatbot to analyze and process individual parts of the input text.
   - **Example:**
     - Input: "How are you?"
     - Tokens: ["How", "are", "you", "?"]

2. **Stopword Removal:**
   - **What It Is:** Stopwords are common words like "is," "the," "on," and "in," which don't carry significant

meaning and are often removed from text before processing.

- o **Why It Matters:** Removing stopwords helps to focus on the important content of the user's message and improves the efficiency of the chatbot.

3. **Stemming and Lemmatization:**
   - o **What They Are:** Both stemming and lemmatization are techniques for reducing words to their base or root form. Stemming simply chops off the ends of words, while lemmatization involves using a dictionary to map a word to its base form.
   - o **Why They Matter:** These techniques help normalize words to their root form, making it easier for the chatbot to understand different forms of a word as one.
   - o **Example:**
     - "running" → "run" (using lemmatization)
     - "better" → "good" (using lemmatization)

4. **Named Entity Recognition (NER):**
   - o **What It Is:** NER is a process of identifying and classifying entities (such as names, dates, locations, and organizations) in text.
   - o **Why It Matters:** Recognizing entities in the text allows the chatbot to understand more specific

details about a user's query, like recognizing names or locations in a question.

- o **Example:**
  - Input: "I want to book a flight to Paris on March 1st."
  - Entities: Paris (Location), March 1st (Date)

5. **Part-of-Speech Tagging (POS):**

- o **What It Is:** POS tagging is the process of labeling each word in a sentence with its grammatical role (e.g., noun, verb, adjective, etc.).
- o **Why It Matters:** POS tagging helps the chatbot understand sentence structure and distinguish between different word types, improving its ability to interpret meaning.
- o **Example:**
  - Input: "I love programming."
  - Tags: "I" (Pronoun), "love" (Verb), "programming" (Noun)

6. **Sentiment Analysis:**

- o **What It Is:** Sentiment analysis is the process of determining the emotional tone of a piece of text (positive, negative, or neutral).
- o **Why It Matters:** For chatbots, understanding the sentiment behind a user's message can help generate

appropriate responses. For example, a chatbot can provide empathy if a user expresses frustration.

- o **Example:**
  - Input: "I am so frustrated with this issue!" → Sentiment: Negative

7. **Word Embeddings (Word2Vec, GloVe):**
   - o **What They Are:** Word embeddings are a technique for converting words into numerical vectors based on their meaning and context in a corpus of text. Word2Vec and GloVe are popular algorithms for generating word embeddings.
   - o **Why They Matter:** Word embeddings allow chatbots to understand relationships between words, such as synonyms, and make sense of words in different contexts.
   - o **Example:** Words like "king" and "queen" would be placed close to each other in the vector space because they are related concepts.

Tools and Libraries for NLP in Python

There are several Python libraries that facilitate the implementation of NLP techniques in chatbot development. Some of the most widely used libraries include:

1. **NLTK (Natural Language Toolkit):**

o **Overview:** NLTK is one of the most comprehensive libraries for NLP in Python. It offers tools for text processing, including tokenization, stemming, POS tagging, and more.

o **Installation:**

bash

```
pip install nltk
```

o **Use Case:** NLTK is ideal for learning and experimenting with NLP concepts, providing a wide array of pre-built functions and corpora for training models.

2. **SpaCy:**

o **Overview:** SpaCy is a modern, high-performance NLP library designed for large-scale applications. It supports various NLP tasks, including tokenization, lemmatization, POS tagging, and named entity recognition.

o **Installation:**

bash

```
pip install spacy
```

o **Use Case:** SpaCy is a go-to library for production-level NLP tasks. It's known for its speed and efficiency when handling large datasets.

3. **TextBlob:**

   o **Overview:** TextBlob is a simpler library built on top of NLTK and Pattern, designed for easy-to-use NLP tasks. It supports common NLP tasks such as sentiment analysis, POS tagging, and noun phrase extraction.

   o **Installation:**

   bash

   pip install textblob

   o **Use Case:** TextBlob is perfect for quick prototyping and basic NLP tasks.

4. **Gensim:**

   o **Overview:** Gensim is a library focused on topic modeling and document similarity. It includes features for working with word embeddings and building topic models.

   o **Installation:**

   bash

   pip install gensim

o **Use Case:** Gensim is widely used for training word embeddings like Word2Vec and for document similarity tasks.

5. **Transformers (by Hugging Face):**

o **Overview:** Hugging Face's Transformers library provides access to state-of-the-art transformer models like BERT, GPT, and T5 for tasks like text generation, question answering, and more.

o **Installation:**

bash

```
pip install transformers
```

o **Use Case:** If you're building a chatbot that requires advanced language understanding, like a generative chatbot, this library is highly useful.

6. **Pattern:**

o **Overview:** Pattern is a library that provides tools for NLP, machine learning, and data mining. It includes modules for text classification, sentiment analysis, and network analysis.

o **Installation:**

bash

```
pip install pattern
```

○ **Use Case:** Pattern is useful for beginners who need an easy-to-use tool for basic NLP and machine learning tasks.

NLP techniques are essential for creating chatbots that understand and generate human language in a meaningful way. By using tools like NLTK, SpaCy, and Transformer-based models, you can equip your chatbot with advanced language processing capabilities, enabling it to perform tasks like sentiment analysis, intent recognition, and dynamic conversation management. Understanding these fundamental NLP techniques and libraries will serve as the foundation for building a chatbot that can effectively interact with users.

Chapter 4: Understanding Intent Recognition

What Are Intents in Chatbot Conversations?

Intents refer to the goals or purposes behind a user's input in a conversation with a chatbot. In other words, an intent is what the user wants to achieve or express by sending a particular message. For example, if a user says "I want to book a flight," the intent is to book a flight. If the user asks "What is the weather today?" the intent is to get weather information.

In a chatbot, recognizing the user's intent is a crucial task because it determines how the bot should respond. The chatbot must be able to understand the intent behind each user query to provide relevant, accurate responses.

Some common examples of intents in chatbot conversations include:

- **Booking a flight**
- **Getting weather information**
- **Making a purchase**
- **Checking account balance**
- **Asking for product recommendations**

For effective chatbot development, it's important to train the bot to identify a range of intents and match user inputs with the appropriate intent. This allows the chatbot to handle diverse interactions, offering contextually appropriate responses.

Introduction to Intent Classification

Intent classification is the process by which a chatbot analyzes a user's message (query) and determines the user's intent. It is a core component of any chatbot using natural language understanding (NLU). Once the intent is classified, the chatbot can trigger the correct response or action.

Intent classification typically involves the following steps:

1. **Text Preprocessing:** The user's input (message) is preprocessed, which includes tokenization, stopword removal, and other NLP techniques.

2. **Feature Extraction:** Features are extracted from the message that will help classify the intent. These features can be keywords, word embeddings, or other meaningful representations of the message.

3. **Model Training:** A machine learning model is trained on a labeled dataset of user messages and their corresponding intents. The model learns to predict the intent based on the input features.

4. **Intent Prediction:** When a new user message arrives, the trained model predicts the intent based on the features extracted from the input message.

5. **Response Generation:** The chatbot generates a response based on the predicted intent, either by following predefined rules or by using an AI model to generate dynamic responses.

To implement intent classification effectively, it's important to have a dataset containing examples of various intents, as this will allow the model to learn patterns and associations between user inputs and intents.

Implementing Intent Recognition in Python

Implementing intent recognition typically involves training a machine learning model, using libraries such as scikit-learn, TensorFlow, or Keras. Here's a simple approach using scikit-learn and a small dataset to classify intents.

1. Preparing the Dataset

The dataset for intent classification consists of examples of user inputs and their corresponding intents. Here's a small example of what such a dataset might look like:

Text	Intent
"Book a flight to New York"	Book_Flight
"What is the weather like today?"	Weather_Request
"Show me the available hotels"	Hotel_Request

Text	Intent
"I need help with my order"	Customer_Support
"What's the stock price of Apple?"	Stock_Request

2. Text Preprocessing

Before training the model, the text data must be preprocessed. This includes tokenization, converting text to lowercase, removing stopwords, and potentially applying lemmatization or stemming.

Here's how you can preprocess the data using nltk:

python

```
import nltk
from nltk.tokenize import word_tokenize
from nltk.corpus import stopwords
from nltk.stem import WordNetLemmatizer

# Download necessary resources
nltk.download('punkt')
nltk.download('stopwords')
nltk.download('wordnet')

# Initialize lemmatizer and stopwords list
lemmatizer = WordNetLemmatizer()
stop_words = set(stopwords.words('english'))

def preprocess_text(text):
```

```
# Tokenize the text
words = word_tokenize(text.lower())
# Remove stopwords and lemmatize each word
return [lemmatizer.lemmatize(word) for word in words if word not in stop_words]
```

```
# Example preprocessing
example_text = "Book a flight to New York"
preprocessed_text = preprocess_text(example_text)
print(preprocessed_text)
```

3. Feature Extraction

In this step, we convert the preprocessed text into a numerical representation that a machine learning model can understand. One common approach is to use a **bag-of-words** model, where each word in the vocabulary is represented by a feature. Alternatively, you can use more advanced techniques like word embeddings (e.g., Word2Vec).

Using CountVectorizer from scikit-learn to implement bag-of-words:

python

```
from sklearn.feature_extraction.text import CountVectorizer
```

```
# Sample data
texts = [
    "Book a flight to New York",
    "What is the weather like today?",
    "Show me the available hotels",
```

    "I need help with my order",

    "What's the stock price of Apple?"

]

labels = ['Book_Flight', 'Weather_Request', 'Hotel_Request', 'Customer_Support', 'Stock_Request']

```
# Initialize CountVectorizer
vectorizer = CountVectorizer()


# Transform the text data into a bag-of-words representation
X = vectorizer.fit_transform(texts)


print(X.toarray())  # Numeric representation of the texts
```

4. Training the Model

Once the features are extracted, you can train a classification model to predict the intent. Here's an example using a **Naive Bayes** classifier:

python

```
from sklearn.naive_bayes import MultinomialNB
from sklearn.model_selection import train_test_split
from sklearn.metrics import accuracy_score


# Split data into training and testing sets
X_train, X_test, y_train, y_test = train_test_split(X, labels, test_size=0.2, random_state=42)


# Train Naive Bayes classifier
```

```
classifier = MultinomialNB()
classifier.fit(X_train, y_train)

# Make predictions on test data
y_pred = classifier.predict(X_test)

# Evaluate the model's performance
print(f'Accuracy: {accuracy_score(y_test, y_pred)}')
```

5. Predicting Intents

After training the model, you can use it to predict the intent of a new user message:

python

```
def predict_intent(text):
    preprocessed_text = preprocess_text(text)
    vectorized_text = vectorizer.transform([' '.join(preprocessed_text)])
    predicted_intent = classifier.predict(vectorized_text)
    return predicted_intent[0]

# Example prediction
user_input = "I want to know the weather today"
predicted_intent = predict_intent(user_input)
print(f'Predicted Intent: {predicted_intent}')
```

6. Fine-Tuning the Model

To improve the chatbot's accuracy in recognizing intents, you can:

- **Expand the dataset:** Include more examples of each intent to help the model learn better.

- **Use word embeddings:** Use pre-trained word embeddings (such as Word2Vec or GloVe) to provide richer representations of words.

- **Try different models:** Experiment with other classification algorithms, such as Support Vector Machines (SVMs) or neural networks, for potentially better performance.

Intent recognition is a vital aspect of chatbot development, allowing the bot to understand what users are trying to achieve. By using text preprocessing, feature extraction, and machine learning models, you can build an intent classifier that makes your chatbot more interactive and intelligent. With Python and libraries like scikit-learn, nltk, and TensorFlow, you can implement intent recognition efficiently and create a chatbot that can handle a wide range of user interactions.

Chapter 5: Building Your First Rule-based Chatbot

In this chapter, we'll walk through the process of building a simple **rule-based chatbot** using Python. A rule-based chatbot responds to user inputs based on predefined rules. These rules are typically defined as conditions (if-else statements) that match user inputs to specific responses. This type of chatbot doesn't use machine learning or NLP but relies on a simple, straightforward logic flow.

We'll also cover **input validation** and how to ensure that the bot handles unexpected inputs in a graceful manner.

Step-by-Step Guide to Building a Simple Rule-based Chatbot

Let's start by creating a simple chatbot that can handle a few basic queries. The chatbot will greet users, provide information about the weather, tell the time, and offer help.

Step 1: Define the Chatbot's Purpose and Responses

First, we'll define the chatbot's goals. In this case, it will handle:

- Greeting the user
- Providing the weather (we will simulate this)
- Providing the current time (simulated)
- Offering help or an exit option

We'll use **if-else statements** to match user input to the appropriate response.

python

```python
import time

# Define the function that returns chatbot's responses based on user input
def chatbot_response(user_input):
    # Convert the input to lowercase for easier matching
    user_input = user_input.lower()

    if "hello" in user_input or "hi" in user_input:
        return "Hello! How can I assist you today?"

    elif "weather" in user_input:
        return "The weather is sunny and warm today!"

    elif "time" in user_input:
        current_time = time.strftime("%H:%M:%S")  # Get current time
        return f"The current time is {current_time}."

    elif "help" in user_input:
        return "I can help you with weather updates or the current time. Just ask!"

    elif "bye" in user_input or "exit" in user_input:
        return "Goodbye! Have a great day."

    else:
        return "Sorry, I didn't understand that. Can you ask something else?"
```

```python
# Main loop to interact with the user
def start_chatbot():
    print("Chatbot: Hello! Type 'bye' or 'exit' to end the conversation.")
    while True:
        user_input = input("You: ")  # Get user input
        response = chatbot_response(user_input)  # Get chatbot's response
        print(f"Chatbot: {response}")

        if user_input.lower() in ["bye", "exit"]:
            break

# Start the chatbot
start_chatbot()
```

Explanation:

1. **chatbot_response(user_input):** This function takes the user's input, converts it to lowercase (to ensure case-insensitivity), and matches the input to predefined conditions. It then returns an appropriate response based on the condition met.

2. **start_chatbot():** This function runs the chatbot in a loop, continuously asking for user input and displaying the chatbot's response until the user types "bye" or "exit".

Step 2: Input Validation and Handling Unexpected Inputs

In the chatbot above, we handle unexpected inputs with a default message: "Sorry, I didn't understand that. Can you ask something else?"

However, we can further enhance input validation to ensure that the user provides a valid query.

For example, if the user enters an empty string or a query that doesn't match any condition, we can prompt the user to enter a valid input.

Here's how you can enhance the chatbot to validate input more effectively:

python

```python
def chatbot_response(user_input):
    # Check for empty input
    if not user_input.strip():
        return "Please enter a valid query. I can help with weather or time-related questions."

    user_input = user_input.lower()

    if "hello" in user_input or "hi" in user_input:
        return "Hello! How can I assist you today?"

    elif "weather" in user_input:
        return "The weather is sunny and warm today!"

    elif "time" in user_input:
        current_time = time.strftime("%H:%M:%S")  # Get current time
        return f"The current time is {current_time}."

    elif "help" in user_input:
```

```
    return "I can help you with weather updates or the current time. Just ask!"

  elif "bye" in user_input or "exit" in user_input:
    return "Goodbye! Have a great day."

  else:
    return "Sorry, I didn't understand that. Can you ask something else?"

# Main loop to interact with the user
def start_chatbot():
  print("Chatbot: Hello! Type 'bye' or 'exit' to end the conversation.")
  while True:
    user_input = input("You: ")  # Get user input
    response = chatbot_response(user_input) # Get chatbot's response
    print(f"Chatbot: {response}")

    if user_input.lower() in ["bye", "exit"]:
      break

# Start the chatbot
start_chatbot()
```

Enhancements:

1. **Empty Input Validation:** The code now checks if the user input is empty or consists only of spaces (if not user_input.strip()). If it is, the bot asks the user to enter a valid query.

2. **Handling Unexpected Queries:** If the user enters a query that the chatbot doesn't understand, the chatbot will prompt

them with "Sorry, I didn't understand that. Can you ask something else?"

Step 3: Extending the Chatbot's Features

You can extend the functionality of the chatbot by adding more predefined rules to handle different types of queries, such as:

- Providing information about the chatbot (e.g., "What is your name?")
- Answering questions about different topics (e.g., sports scores, news, etc.)
- Incorporating simple calculations (e.g., adding numbers)

Here's an example of extending the chatbot to answer the user's name query:

python

```python
def chatbot_response(user_input):
    # Check for empty input
    if not user_input.strip():
        return "Please enter a valid query. I can help with weather or time-related questions."

    user_input = user_input.lower()

    if "hello" in user_input or "hi" in user_input:
        return "Hello! How can I assist you today?"
```

```python
    elif "weather" in user_input:
        return "The weather is sunny and warm today!"

    elif "time" in user_input:
        current_time = time.strftime("%H:%M:%S")  # Get current time
        return f"The current time is {current_time}."

    elif "help" in user_input:
        return "I can help you with weather updates or the current time. Just ask!"

    elif "name" in user_input:
        return "I am your friendly chatbot!"

    elif "bye" in user_input or "exit" in user_input:
        return "Goodbye! Have a great day."

    else:
        return "Sorry, I didn't understand that. Can you ask something else?"


# Start the chatbot
start_chatbot()
```

Step 4: Improving User Interaction

To make the chatbot more interactive, you can:

- **Use more conversational prompts** to make it feel more human-like.
- **Offer more advanced input validation** to handle different types of errors (e.g., invalid commands or commands with mixed case).

For example, you can modify the chatbot to give suggestions when it doesn't understand the input, like so:

python

```
else:
    return "Sorry, I didn't understand that. Try asking about the weather or the time."
```

In this chapter, we built a basic rule-based chatbot using Python. We also covered input validation to ensure that the chatbot responds appropriately to unexpected or empty inputs. While this type of chatbot is simple and limited to predefined rules, it's a great starting point and a solid foundation for more advanced bots in the future.

Chapter 6: Tokenization and Preprocessing Text Data

In this chapter, we will delve into **text preprocessing**—a critical step in Natural Language Processing (NLP). Preprocessing text is essential for cleaning and preparing raw data before feeding it into an NLP model, like a chatbot. This chapter will cover the importance of text preprocessing, key techniques like tokenization, stemming, and lemmatization, and Python libraries that can help with these tasks.

Importance of Text Preprocessing in NLP

Text preprocessing is crucial in NLP because raw text data is often unstructured, noisy, and inconsistent. Before we can use the data for any NLP tasks (e.g., sentiment analysis, intent classification, chatbot interactions), it must be cleaned and structured in a way that allows a model to understand it.

Why Text Preprocessing Matters:

1. **Noise Reduction:** Raw text often contains irrelevant information (such as punctuation, special characters, or extraneous whitespace) that can negatively affect the performance of NLP models.
2. **Consistency:** Preprocessing makes the text uniform, which helps NLP algorithms perform better by reducing

inconsistencies. For instance, converting all text to lowercase makes the model case-insensitive.

3. **Tokenization:** It breaks down large text bodies into smaller, meaningful components (tokens), allowing easier analysis.

4. **Feature Extraction:** Preprocessing helps to extract features (such as word frequencies or relationships) that are meaningful for machine learning algorithms.

The main steps involved in preprocessing text include **tokenization, removing stopwords, stemming, lemmatization**, and more. Let's explore these techniques in detail.

Techniques: Tokenization, Stemming, and Lemmatization

1. **Tokenization**

   o **What Is Tokenization?** Tokenization is the process of breaking down text into smaller units, called tokens. These tokens can be words, sentences, or subword units.

   o **Why Is Tokenization Important?** Tokenization helps transform raw text into meaningful components (words or phrases), which makes it easier to analyze the text. For example, "I am happy" would be tokenized into three tokens: ["I", "am", "happy"].

   o **Types of Tokenization:**

- **Word Tokenization:** Splitting text into words (e.g., "I am happy" becomes ["I", "am", "happy"]).
- **Sentence Tokenization:** Splitting text into sentences (e.g., "I am happy. How are you?" becomes ["I am happy.", "How are you?"]).

Example (Word Tokenization with nltk):

python

```
import nltk
from nltk.tokenize import word_tokenize

nltk.download('punkt')  # Download the punkt tokenizer model

text = "I am learning Natural Language Processing!"
tokens = word_tokenize(text)
print(tokens)
# Output: ['I', 'am', 'learning', 'Natural', 'Language', 'Processing', '!']
```

2. **Stemming**

   o **What Is Stemming?** Stemming is the process of reducing words to their root or base form by chopping off prefixes or suffixes. It is a simple technique that removes variations of words (e.g., "running" → "run").

○ **Why Is Stemming Important?** Stemming is useful when you want to group similar words and reduce the number of unique terms in the dataset. However, stemming is a heuristic process, which means it may sometimes produce incorrect or incomplete root forms.

Example (Stemming with nltk):

python

```
from nltk.stem import PorterStemmer

stemmer = PorterStemmer()

words = ["running", "runner", "runs", "ran"]
stemmed_words = [stemmer.stem(word) for word in words]
print(stemmed_words)
# Output: ['run', 'runner', 'run', 'ran']
```

3. **Lemmatization**

○ **What Is Lemmatization?** Lemmatization is a more advanced technique than stemming. It reduces words to their base or dictionary form (lemma) using a vocabulary and morphological analysis of the word. Unlike stemming, lemmatization ensures that the result is a valid word.

o **Why Is Lemmatization Important?**
Lemmatization is more accurate than stemming because it considers the context of the word (e.g., "better" → "good"). It is ideal for tasks where the semantic meaning of the word is essential, such as in chatbots and text classification.

Example (Lemmatization with nltk):

python

```
from nltk.stem import WordNetLemmatizer
from nltk.corpus import wordnet

nltk.download('wordnet')  # Download the WordNet corpus

lemmatizer = WordNetLemmatizer()

words = ["running", "better", "cats"]
lemmatized_words          =          [lemmatizer.lemmatize(word,
pos=wordnet.VERB) for word in words]
print(lemmatized_words)
# Output: ['run', 'better', 'cat']
```

Key Difference Between Stemming and Lemmatization:

o **Stemming** cuts off prefixes or suffixes to find the root of the word.

- **Lemmatization** uses linguistic rules and a dictionary to convert words into their valid root form based on their context.

Python Libraries for Text Preprocessing

Python offers several powerful libraries for text preprocessing. Some of the most commonly used libraries are:

1. **NLTK (Natural Language Toolkit)**
   - **Overview:** NLTK is one of the most popular libraries for NLP in Python. It provides a wide range of text preprocessing functionalities, including tokenization, stopword removal, stemming, lemmatization, and more.
   - **Installation:**

   bash

   ```
   pip install nltk
   ```

   - **Use Case:** NLTK is a great library for educational purposes and for building simpler text preprocessing pipelines.

2. **SpaCy**
   - **Overview:** SpaCy is a more efficient and modern library for NLP tasks, including tokenization, lemmatization, dependency parsing, and named

entity recognition. It is designed for production use and is faster than NLTK.

- o **Installation:**

  bash

  pip install spacy

- o **Use Case:** SpaCy is well-suited for large-scale NLP tasks and production-level applications.

Example of Lemmatization with SpaCy:

python

import spacy

```
# Load the SpaCy model
nlp = spacy.load("en_core_web_sm")

text = "The cats are running faster."
doc = nlp(text)

lemmatized_words = [token.lemma_ for token in doc]
print(lemmatized_words)
# Output: ['the', 'cat', 'be', 'run', 'faster']
```

3. **TextBlob**
   - o **Overview:** TextBlob is a simple library built on top of NLTK and Pattern, and it is known for its ease of

use. It supports basic NLP tasks such as tokenization, part-of-speech tagging, and sentiment analysis.

o **Installation:**

bash

pip install textblob

o **Use Case:** TextBlob is ideal for beginners who need a simple interface for basic NLP tasks.

Example of Tokenization and Lemmatization with TextBlob:

python

from textblob import Word

```
word = Word("running")
print(word.lemmatize("v"))  # Lemmatizes 'running' to 'run'
```

4. **Gensim**

o **Overview:** Gensim is another popular library primarily used for topic modeling and document similarity analysis. It also includes implementations of word embeddings (Word2Vec, FastText).

o **Installation:**

bash

pip install gensim

- o **Use Case:** Gensim is ideal for projects involving word embeddings or document similarity.

5. **Scikit-learn**

- o **Overview:** Scikit-learn provides utilities for text feature extraction, such as converting text to numerical representations (e.g., bag-of-words, TF-IDF). It is often used in conjunction with machine learning models.

- o **Installation:**

bash

pip install scikit-learn

- o **Use Case:** Scikit-learn is used for machine learning pipelines that involve feature extraction from text.

Text preprocessing is a crucial step in NLP that transforms raw text into a structured and meaningful form for further analysis. Techniques like **tokenization**, **stemming**, and **lemmatization** are vital for cleaning and preparing text data. Python libraries like **NLTK, SpaCy, TextBlob,** and **Gensim** provide powerful tools for these tasks, making it easier to build robust and accurate NLP models.

Chapter 7: Working with Regular Expressions for NLP

Regular expressions (regex) are a powerful tool in programming for matching patterns in text. They play an important role in many tasks in natural language processing (NLP) and chatbot development, such as identifying specific words or phrases, validating input, and extracting data from text.

In this chapter, we will explore what regular expressions are, how they can be used in chatbots for pattern matching, and provide practical examples of their use in chatbot development.

What Are Regular Expressions?

A **regular expression** is a sequence of characters that forms a search pattern. Regular expressions allow you to perform complex text searches and manipulations by defining a pattern that can match a set of strings. This makes them invaluable for text processing tasks in NLP and chatbot development.

Key Components of Regular Expressions:

- **Literal characters:** Regular characters that match themselves in the text. For example, "hello" will match the string "hello" in the text.
- **Metacharacters:** Special characters with specific meanings, used to define patterns. Common metacharacters include:

o . (dot): Matches any single character except newline.

o ^: Matches the beginning of a string.

o $: Matches the end of a string.

o *: Matches zero or more of the preceding character or group.

o +: Matches one or more of the preceding character or group.

o ?: Matches zero or one of the preceding character or group.

o []: Defines a character class to match any one character within the brackets.

o |: Acts as a logical OR.

o () : Groups patterns together.

Regular expressions are supported in Python through the re module, which provides functions to search for patterns, replace text, and split strings.

How to Use Regular Expressions in Chatbots for Pattern Matching

In chatbot development, regular expressions can be used for tasks such as:

- **Intent matching:** Matching patterns in user input to trigger specific responses (e.g., recognizing greetings, commands, or questions).

- **Input validation:** Ensuring user input follows a specific format (e.g., validating phone numbers or email addresses).
- **Keyword extraction:** Extracting specific information from the user's input (e.g., dates, locations, or product names).

Here's an overview of how to use the re module in Python to work with regular expressions:

1. **re.match():** Checks if the regular expression matches at the beginning of the string.
2. **re.search():** Searches for the first location where the regular expression pattern matches anywhere in the string.
3. **re.findall():** Returns a list of all non-overlapping matches of the pattern in the string.
4. **re.sub():** Replaces occurrences of the pattern with a specified replacement string.

Let's now look at some examples of using regular expressions for pattern matching in chatbot development.

Examples in Chatbot Development

1. **Greeting Detection:**

In a chatbot, you might want to detect when a user greets the bot. A regular expression can help match greetings like "Hello", "Hi", or "Hey".

Example Code:

python

```
import re

# Define a function to detect greetings
def detect_greeting(user_input):
    greetings = r"^(hello|hi|hey|greetings|howdy)"
    if re.match(greetings, user_input, re.IGNORECASE):
        return "Hello! How can I help you today?"
    else:
        return "I didn't catch that. Please say 'hello' to start a conversation."

# Test the function
user_input = "Hey, what's up?"
print(detect_greeting(user_input))  # Output: Hello! How can I help you today?

user_input = "How are you?"
print(detect_greeting(user_input))  # Output: I didn't catch that. Please say 'hello'
to start a conversation.
```

In this example, the regular expression r"^(hello|hi|hey|greetings|howdy)" matches any greeting at the beginning of the user input, regardless of case (thanks to re.IGNORECASE).

2. Extracting Dates from User Input:

If you want your chatbot to recognize and extract dates from user input, you can use regular expressions to find date patterns like "June 5th", "12/05/2025", or "5th of June".

Example Code:

python

```
import re

# Define a function to extract dates
def extract_date(user_input):
    # Regular expression pattern for dates
    date_pattern = r"\b(\d{1,2}[-/th|st|nd|rd]*\s*(?:of\s*)?[A-Za-z]+\s*\d{2,4})\b"
    matches = re.findall(date_pattern, user_input)

    if matches:
        return f"Found date(s): {matches}"
    else:
        return "No dates found."

# Test the function
user_input = "I have a meeting on 12/05/2025 and another on 5th of June."
print(extract_date(user_input))  # Output: Found date(s): ['12/05/2025', '5th of June']

user_input = "Let's meet next week."
print(extract_date(user_input))  # Output: No dates found.
```

In this case, the regular expression pattern r"\b(\d{1,2}[-/th|st|nd|rd]*\s*(?:of\s*)?[A-Za-z]+\s*\d{2,4})\b" matches a variety of date formats, including those with ordinal suffixes like "5th" or "12nd".

3. Validating Email Addresses:

If your chatbot needs to validate an email address provided by the user, regular expressions can be used to check if the input matches the structure of a valid email address.

Example Code:

python

```python
import re

# Define a function to validate email
def validate_email(user_input):
    email_pattern = r"^[a-zA-Z0-9_.+-]+@[a-zA-Z0-9-]+\.[a-zA-Z0-9-.]+$"
    if re.match(email_pattern, user_input):
        return "Valid email address."
    else:
        return "Invalid email address."

# Test the function
user_input = "test@example.com"
print(validate_email(user_input))  # Output: Valid email address.

user_input = "invalid-email@com"
print(validate_email(user_input))  # Output: Invalid email address.
```

Here, the regular expression r"^[a-zA-Z0-9_.+-]+@[a-zA-Z0-9-]+\.[a-zA-Z0-9-.]+$" matches a typical email address pattern, validating that the input has the correct format.

4. **Matching Commands or Keywords:**

A chatbot often needs to identify specific commands or keywords within user input, such as "help", "cancel", or "status". Regular expressions can be used to detect these keywords in a flexible way.

Example Code:

python

```
import re

# Define a function to match commands
def process_command(user_input):
    # Regular expression to match commands
    command_pattern = r"\b(help|cancel|status|order)\b"
    match = re.search(command_pattern, user_input, re.IGNORECASE)

    if match:
        return f"Command '{match.group()}' detected. Processing..."
    else:
        return "No valid command detected."

# Test the function
user_input = "Can you please help me?"
print(process_command(user_input))    # Output: Command 'help' detected.
Processing...

user_input = "I want to cancel my order."
print(process_command(user_input))    # Output: Command 'cancel' detected.
Processing...
```

In this case, r"\b(help|cancel|status|order)\b" matches any of the listed keywords, ensuring that the chatbot can react to these commands.

Regular expressions are an invaluable tool for chatbots, enabling tasks like pattern matching, input validation, and data extraction. They can help a chatbot understand a wide variety of user inputs, from greetings and dates to commands and email addresses. By using the re module in Python, you can implement powerful and flexible pattern matching that enhances the user experience.

Chapter 8: Understanding Named Entity Recognition (NER)

In this chapter, we will explore **Named Entity Recognition (NER)**, its importance in chatbot development, and how to implement it in Python using popular libraries like **SpaCy** and **NLTK**. NER is a crucial NLP task that allows chatbots to identify and classify key pieces of information (entities) from user input, such as names, dates, locations, organizations, and more.

What is NER and Its Role in Chatbots?

Named Entity Recognition (NER) is a process in Natural Language Processing (NLP) that identifies and classifies named entities in a text into predefined categories. These entities could be:

- **Persons** (e.g., "John Doe")
- **Organizations** (e.g., "Google", "Apple")
- **Locations** (e.g., "Paris", "New York")
- **Dates and Times** (e.g., "January 1st", "next Monday")
- **Monetary values** (e.g., "$100", "€50")

The role of NER in chatbots is significant because it allows the bot to:

- **Understand user input better** by recognizing important details (such as a person's name or a specific location).

- **Generate context-aware responses**, which helps create a more interactive and personalized experience for the user.

- **Extract specific information** to respond to user queries. For instance, if a user asks, "What's the weather in Paris tomorrow?", the chatbot needs to extract "Paris" as the location to fetch the correct weather information.

For example, if a user says: "I want to book a flight to Paris next Tuesday," a chatbot with NER capabilities will identify "Paris" as a **Location** and "next Tuesday" as a **Date**. This allows the bot to process the request correctly.

Implementing NER in Python

There are several Python libraries that make it easy to implement NER, with **SpaCy** and **NLTK** being two of the most popular ones. Let's look at how to use each library for Named Entity Recognition.

Using SpaCy for NER

SpaCy is an industrial-strength NLP library designed for performance and ease of use. It provides a built-in NER pipeline that can automatically detect entities in text. Let's see how to implement NER with SpaCy.

Step 1: Install and Load the SpaCy Model

First, you need to install the SpaCy library and download the pre-trained model that includes NER capabilities.

bash

pip install spacy
python -m spacy download en_core_web_sm

Step 2: Using SpaCy for Named Entity Recognition

python

```python
import spacy

# Load the pre-trained SpaCy model for NER
nlp = spacy.load("en_core_web_sm")

# Process the text
text = "Apple is planning to launch a new iPhone model in Paris on January 15th, 2025."
doc = nlp(text)

# Extract named entities
for entity in doc.ents:
    print(f"{entity.text} ({entity.label_})")
```

Output:

scss

```
Apple (ORG)
Paris (GPE)
January 15th, 2025 (DATE)
```

Explanation:

- **en_core_web_sm** is a pre-trained SpaCy model that includes a variety of NLP components, including a Named Entity Recognition model.
- The **doc.ents** property of a SpaCy document object contains all detected entities. Each entity is represented as a **Span** object that contains the entity text and its associated label (e.g., "ORG" for organization, "GPE" for geographical location, "DATE" for dates).

Step 3: Custom NER (Optional)

SpaCy also allows you to train a custom NER model for specific entities that may not be captured by the general-purpose model. This is useful if you want to detect specialized entities, such as product names or customer IDs, in your chatbot interactions.

python

```
# Add a custom NER rule (this is just an illustrative example)
from spacy.training import Example

# Define new data for training the NER model
TRAIN_DATA = [
    ("I visited Google in Mountain View.", {"entities": [(10, 16, "ORG"), (20, 33, "GPE")]}),
    ("My friend's birthday is on March 15th.", {"entities": [(19, 30, "DATE")]}),
]

# Create an empty model or load an existing one and train it
```

```
ner = nlp.create_pipe("ner")
nlp.add_pipe(ner, last=True)
for text, annotations in TRAIN_DATA:
    doc = nlp.make_doc(text)
    example = Example.from_dict(doc, annotations)
    nlp.update([example])
```

This code demonstrates how to train SpaCy to recognize custom entities. You would typically use this approach for a chatbot that handles industry-specific terms or personalized data.

Using NLTK for NER

NLTK (Natural Language Toolkit) is another popular library for NLP tasks, including NER. It also has a built-in function for recognizing named entities, but it generally requires external resources like **punkt** for tokenization and **maxent_ne_chunker** for entity recognition.

Step 1: Install NLTK and Download Resources

bash

```
pip install nltk
```

You'll need to download additional NLTK data sets:

python

```
import nltk
nltk.download('punkt')
nltk.download('maxent_ne_chunker')
nltk.download('words')
```

Step 2: Using NLTK for Named Entity Recognition

python

```python
import nltk
from nltk import word_tokenize, pos_tag, ne_chunk

# Sample text for NER
text = "Apple is planning to launch a new iPhone model in Paris on January 15th, 2025."

# Tokenize and POS tag
words = word_tokenize(text)
tags = pos_tag(words)

# Apply Named Entity Recognition
tree = ne_chunk(tags)

# Print the entities
for subtree in tree:
    if isinstance(subtree, nltk.Tree):
        entity = " ".join([word for word, tag in subtree])
        label = subtree.label()
        print(f"{entity} ({label})")
```

Output:

scss

```
Apple (GPE)
Paris (GPE)
January 15th, 2025 (DATE)
```

77

Explanation:

- **Tokenization and POS tagging** are the first steps, where the text is broken down into words, and each word is tagged with a part of speech (POS).
- `ne_chunk` performs named entity recognition by identifying entities in the POS-tagged words.
- The result is a nested tree structure, where each leaf node corresponds to a word, and each subtree corresponds to a named entity (e.g., "Apple" is a **GPE** – Geopolitical Entity).

Advantages and Limitations of SpaCy and NLTK for NER

- **SpaCy**:
    - o **Advantages:** Faster and more efficient for large-scale text processing; pre-trained models are highly accurate; easy to use for both beginners and advanced users.
    - o **Limitations:** Limited flexibility for fine-tuning without training custom models; pre-trained models may not always capture domain-specific entities.
- **NLTK**:
    - o **Advantages:** Highly flexible and configurable; great for learning and educational purposes; easy to combine with other NLP tasks.

- ○ **Limitations:** Less efficient for large-scale tasks; the pre-trained NER model is less accurate compared to SpaCy's models.

Named Entity Recognition (NER) is an essential technique in chatbot development, as it helps identify important pieces of information in user input, such as names, locations, and dates. By using libraries like **SpaCy** and **NLTK**, you can easily implement NER in your chatbot, enabling it to handle more sophisticated conversations and provide more personalized responses.

Chapter 9: Building a Simple NLP Model

In this chapter, we will walk through the process of building a **simple NLP model** for text classification. Text classification is an essential NLP task where the goal is to assign predefined categories (labels) to text. For instance, a chatbot might classify user queries into categories like "greeting," "weather," or "product inquiry." We will use **scikit-learn**, a popular Python library for machine learning, to build a text classification model and evaluate its performance.

Training a Machine Learning Model for NLP Tasks

To build an NLP model for text classification, we need to follow these main steps:

1. **Prepare the dataset**: We need labeled data (texts and their corresponding labels).

2. **Preprocess the text data**: Text data needs to be cleaned and transformed into a format suitable for machine learning models.

3. **Feature extraction**: Convert the text data into numerical features that can be fed into machine learning algorithms.

4. **Model training**: Train a machine learning model on the transformed text data.

5. **Model evaluation**: Evaluate the performance of the trained model.

Let's walk through each of these steps.

Step 1: Prepare the Dataset

For this example, we'll use a simple dataset of text samples with corresponding labels. This dataset might represent different types of queries a chatbot might handle, such as greetings or weather inquiries.

Example Dataset:

Text	Label
"Hello, how are you?"	Greeting
"What is the weather like today?"	Weather
"Can you help me with my order?"	Customer_Support
"What's the temperature in Paris?"	Weather
"Good morning, are you there?"	Greeting
"I need help with my account"	Customer_Support

We will use this dataset to train a simple text classification model.

Step 2: Preprocess the Text Data

Before we can train the model, we need to preprocess the text data. Common preprocessing steps for text include:

- **Lowercasing**: Convert all text to lowercase to ensure case insensitivity.
- **Tokenization**: Split text into words or tokens.
- **Removing stopwords**: Eliminate common words (e.g., "and," "the") that do not carry significant meaning.
- **Lemmatization or stemming**: Reduce words to their base or root form.

Here is how you can preprocess the text data using Python:

python

```python
import nltk
from nltk.corpus import stopwords
from nltk.tokenize import word_tokenize
from nltk.stem import WordNetLemmatizer

# Download necessary NLTK resources
nltk.download('punkt')
nltk.download('stopwords')
nltk.download('wordnet')

# Initialize the lemmatizer and stopwords list
lemmatizer = WordNetLemmatizer()
stop_words = set(stopwords.words('english'))
```

```
# Preprocessing function
def preprocess_text(text):
    # Tokenize the text
    words = word_tokenize(text.lower())  # Convert to lowercase and tokenize
    # Remove stopwords and lemmatize each word
    return [lemmatizer.lemmatize(word) for word in words if word not in
stop_words]
```

```
# Example preprocessing
text = "What is the weather like today?"
preprocessed_text = preprocess_text(text)
print(preprocessed_text)
```

Step 3: Feature Extraction

Machine learning models work with numerical data, so we need to convert our text data into numerical features. A common technique for feature extraction in NLP is **Bag-of-Words (BoW)**. This method converts the text into a matrix of token counts, where each column represents a word and each row represents a document or sentence.

We'll use **CountVectorizer** from scikit-learn to implement this:

python

```
from sklearn.feature_extraction.text import CountVectorizer
```

```
# Example dataset
texts = [
    "Hello, how are you?",
```

```
    "What is the weather like today?",
    "Can you help me with my order?",
    "What's the temperature in Paris?",
    "Good morning, are you there?",
    "I need help with my account"
]
labels = ['Greeting', 'Weather', 'Customer_Support', 'Weather', 'Greeting',
'Customer_Support']

# Initialize the CountVectorizer
vectorizer = CountVectorizer(stop_words='english')

# Fit the model and transform the text into feature vectors
X = vectorizer.fit_transform(texts)

# Show the feature vectors
print(X.toarray())  # Output: matrix of word counts
```

The CountVectorizer transforms each text into a vector where each element represents the count of a specific word in the text.

Step 4: Model Training

Now that we have transformed the text data into numerical features, we can train a machine learning model. We'll use **Multinomial Naive Bayes**, which is commonly used for text classification tasks.

python

```
from sklearn.model_selection import train_test_split
from sklearn.naive_bayes import MultinomialNB
```

```python
from sklearn.metrics import accuracy_score

# Split data into training and test sets
X_train, X_test, y_train, y_test = train_test_split(X, labels, test_size=0.3,
random_state=42)

# Initialize the Naive Bayes classifier
classifier = MultinomialNB()

# Train the model
classifier.fit(X_train, y_train)

# Make predictions on the test set
y_pred = classifier.predict(X_test)

# Evaluate the model
print(f'Accuracy: {accuracy_score(y_test, y_pred)}')
```

In this step, we:

- Split the data into training and testing sets using train_test_split.
- Train a **Multinomial Naive Bayes** model using fit() on the training data.
- Evaluate the model on the test set by calculating the accuracy score.

Step 5: Model Evaluation

Once the model is trained, it is important to evaluate its performance to ensure it is working well. A few common evaluation metrics for classification tasks include:

- **Accuracy**: The proportion of correctly classified instances.
- **Precision**: The proportion of true positive results among all positive results.
- **Recall**: The proportion of true positive results among all actual positives.
- **F1 Score**: The harmonic mean of precision and recall.

python

```python
from sklearn.metrics import classification_report

# Print the classification report
print(classification_report(y_test, y_pred))
```

The classification_report function from scikit-learn provides detailed evaluation metrics, including precision, recall, and F1 score for each class.

Example Output:

markdown

```
Accuracy: 0.8333
          precision   recall  f1-score   support
```

Greeting	1.00	0.75	0.86	1
Weather	0.50	1.00	0.67	1
Customer_Support	0.83	1.00	0.91	1
accuracy		0.83	3	
macro avg	0.78	0.92	0.81	3
weighted avg	0.85	0.83	0.83	3

Here, the **accuracy** is 83.33%, meaning the model correctly classified 83% of the test instances.

In this chapter, we learned how to:

1. **Preprocess text data** to make it suitable for machine learning.
2. **Extract features** from text using **Bag-of-Words**.
3. **Train a text classification model** using **Multinomial Naive Bayes**.
4. **Evaluate the model's performance** using accuracy and other metrics.

By following these steps, you can build your own text classification model for a variety of NLP tasks, such as classifying user queries in a chatbot.

Chapter 10: Advanced NLP Techniques for Chatbots

In this chapter, we will explore **advanced NLP techniques** that enhance the capabilities of chatbots, focusing on **word embeddings**, **Word2Vec**, and **GloVe** models. These techniques help chatbots understand the relationships between words, improve their ability to handle complex conversations, and make their responses more accurate and natural.

What are Word Embeddings and Their Importance?

Word embeddings are a technique for converting words into dense vector representations in a continuous vector space, where similar words are placed closer to each other. Unlike traditional methods like **Bag-of-Words** (BoW), which represent words as discrete counts, word embeddings capture semantic meaning and contextual relationships between words.

Why are Word Embeddings Important for Chatbots?

- **Capturing semantic relationships:** Word embeddings allow chatbots to understand that words like "king" and "queen" are related, or that "Paris" is a city while "dog" is an animal, even if they have never been explicitly taught those relationships.

- **Handling synonyms:** Word embeddings help chatbots recognize that words with similar meanings (e.g., "car" and "automobile") are represented by similar vectors, improving the chatbot's ability to respond to varied phrasing.

- **Reducing dimensionality:** Unlike Bag-of-Words, which can result in high-dimensional, sparse vectors, word embeddings offer a more compact and informative representation of words.

By embedding words into a vector space, chatbots can perform more complex tasks such as sentiment analysis, text generation, and intent recognition. Now, let's dive into two of the most popular word embedding models: **Word2Vec** and **GloVe**.

Word2Vec and GloVe Models

1. **Word2Vec (Word to Vector)**
   - **What Is Word2Vec?** Word2Vec is a shallow neural network model trained to predict words given their context (skip-gram model) or predict context words given a target word (continuous bag-of-words model). It creates dense word embeddings by training on large corpora of text and learning to map words to vectors that reflect their meaning and relationships with other words.
   - **Why is Word2Vec Important?**

- It captures semantic relationships between words, so similar words will have similar vector representations.
- Word2Vec models can be trained on large corpora, and they learn high-quality embeddings that work well for various NLP tasks.

- **How Word2Vec Works:** Word2Vec learns embeddings by using context. For example, in the sentence "The cat sat on the mat," Word2Vec uses the words around "cat" (context) to predict the word "cat." The network is trained to minimize the difference between the predicted and actual target words.

2. **GloVe (Global Vectors for Word Representation)**

- **What Is GloVe?** GloVe is another popular word embedding technique that is based on matrix factorization. Instead of relying on context windows like Word2Vec, GloVe uses global word co-occurrence statistics to construct word embeddings. It builds a word co-occurrence matrix from a large corpus of text and then factors it to generate dense word vectors.

- **Why is GloVe Important?**

- GloVe captures global relationships in a corpus, meaning it uses word co-occurrence information from the entire text to construct its embeddings.
- It provides high-quality embeddings and can be computationally efficient when trained on large text corpora.

  o **How GloVe Works:** GloVe creates a co-occurrence matrix where each entry represents how often two words appear together in the text. The embeddings are learned by factorizing this matrix, which ensures that words with similar meanings have similar vector representations.

Using Pre-trained Word Embeddings in Python

While you can train Word2Vec or GloVe models on your own data, in most cases, it's more practical to use pre-trained embeddings, which have been trained on large corpora and are readily available. These embeddings can be used to improve the performance of your chatbot, especially when you don't have a large amount of training data.

Here's how you can use **pre-trained word embeddings** in Python using the **Gensim** library for Word2Vec and **spaCy** for GloVe.

Using Word2Vec with Gensim

Step 1: Install Gensim

bash

pip install gensim

Step 2: Load a Pre-trained Word2Vec Model

Gensim provides a pre-trained Word2Vec model trained on the Google News dataset. You can load it and use it in your chatbot.

python

```
import gensim.downloader as api

# Load the pre-trained Word2Vec model
model = api.load("word2vec-google-news-300")


# Example: Find the similarity between two words
similarity = model.similarity("king", "queen")
print(f"Similarity between 'king' and 'queen': {similarity}")
```

Step 3: Using Word2Vec for Word Analogies Word2Vec can also be used to solve word analogies, such as "king" is to "queen" as "man" is to "woman."

python

```
# Word analogy example: "king" is to "queen" as "man" is to "woman"
result = model.most_similar(positive=["king", "woman"], negative=["man"], topn=1)
print(f"Analogy result: {result}")
```

Using GloVe with spaCy

92

Step 1: Install spaCy and Download a Pre-trained GloVe Model

You can use **spaCy** to load GloVe embeddings and use them in your NLP tasks.

bash

```
pip install spacy
python -m spacy download en_vectors_web_lg
```

Step 2: Load and Use GloVe Embeddings

python

```python
import spacy

# Load the pre-trained GloVe model (en_vectors_web_lg)
nlp = spacy.load("en_vectors_web_lg")

# Example: Find the similarity between two words
word1 = nlp("king")
word2 = nlp("queen")
similarity = word1.similarity(word2)
print(f"Similarity between 'king' and 'queen': {similarity}")
```

Step 3: Use GloVe Embeddings for Similarity Tasks

You can now use the GloVe embeddings to find word similarities, document similarity, or perform other advanced NLP tasks like clustering and classification.

python

```
# Use similarity to find words related to "king"
similar_words = nlp.vocab.vectors.most_similar(nlp("king").vector, n=5)
print(f"Words similar to 'king': {similar_words}")
```

Advanced Use Cases of Word Embeddings in Chatbots

1. **Intent Classification**: By using word embeddings, chatbots can better classify user intents by understanding the semantic meaning behind words, even if the user uses different synonyms to express the same intent.

2. **Sentiment Analysis**: Word embeddings help chatbots understand the sentiment of a sentence by analyzing the relationship between words, allowing the chatbot to detect positive, negative, or neutral sentiments.

3. **Entity Recognition**: Embeddings can improve the chatbot's ability to recognize named entities, such as names, locations, and dates, even when expressed in different ways.

4. **Contextual Understanding**: Word embeddings can help chatbots understand the context of a conversation. For example, if the chatbot detects a word like "Paris" (a location), it can respond with relevant travel or weather information.

In this chapter, we explored advanced NLP techniques, focusing on **word embeddings** and their importance in building smarter and more efficient chatbots. We examined **Word2Vec** and **GloVe**, two of the most popular word embedding models, and discussed how to use pre-trained embeddings in Python with libraries like **Gensim** and **spaCy**. These embeddings provide chatbots with a deeper understanding of language, enabling them to perform tasks like sentiment analysis, intent classification, and entity recognition with greater accuracy.

Chapter 11: Intent Classification with Machine Learning

In this chapter, we will focus on **intent classification**, which is a crucial task in chatbot development. Intent classification helps the chatbot understand the goal or purpose behind the user's message, enabling it to provide relevant responses. We'll cover how to implement machine learning for intent recognition, compare various machine learning algorithms for this task, and evaluate the model's performance.

Implementing Machine Learning for Intent Recognition

Intent recognition involves classifying user inputs into predefined categories (or intents), such as "greeting," "product inquiry," or "weather query." Machine learning algorithms can be trained to automatically recognize these intents based on patterns in the text.

Here's how to implement intent classification using machine learning in Python:

1. **Prepare the Dataset**: You'll need a labeled dataset consisting of user inputs (queries) and their corresponding intents. For example:

Text	Intent
"Hello, how are you?"	Greeting
"What is the weather like today?"	Weather
"Can I track my order?"	Order_Tracking
"What time does the store close?"	Store_Info
"Hi, I need help with my account"	Customer_Support

2. This dataset will be used to train a machine learning model.

3. **Preprocess the Text**: Text data must be cleaned and transformed into a format that machine learning algorithms can understand. This includes:
   o Tokenization
   o Lowercasing
   o Removing stopwords
   o Lemmatization or stemming

We will use the CountVectorizer or TfidfVectorizer from scikit-learn to convert the text into numerical features (vectors).

4. **Feature Extraction**:
   o **CountVectorizer**: Converts text into a sparse matrix of word counts.

- o **TfidfVectorizer**: Converts text into a sparse matrix of TF-IDF (Term Frequency-Inverse Document Frequency) scores, which downweights common words that appear frequently across all documents.

5. **Training the Model**: Once the text is preprocessed and converted into numerical features, we can train a machine learning model. Common algorithms for intent classification include:
    - o **Logistic Regression**
    - o **Naive Bayes**
    - o **Support Vector Machines (SVM)**
    - o **Random Forests**

Here's how you can implement intent classification using **Naive Bayes**:

python

```
from sklearn.feature_extraction.text import TfidfVectorizer
from sklearn.naive_bayes import MultinomialNB
from sklearn.model_selection import train_test_split
from sklearn.metrics import accuracy_score, classification_report

# Example dataset
texts = [
    "Hello, how are you?",
    "What is the weather like today?",
    "Can I track my order?",
```

"What time does the store close?",

"Hi, I need help with my account"

]

labels = ['Greeting', 'Weather', 'Order_Tracking', 'Store_Info', 'Customer_Support']

```python
# Step 1: Preprocess the text and convert to numerical features using TfidfVectorizer
vectorizer = TfidfVectorizer(stop_words='english')
X = vectorizer.fit_transform(texts)

# Step 2: Split the data into training and testing sets
X_train, X_test, y_train, y_test = train_test_split(X, labels, test_size=0.3, random_state=42)

# Step 3: Train the Naive Bayes model
model = MultinomialNB()
model.fit(X_train, y_train)

# Step 4: Make predictions and evaluate the model
y_pred = model.predict(X_test)

# Evaluate the model
accuracy = accuracy_score(y_test, y_pred)
print(f"Accuracy: {accuracy}")
print("Classification Report:\n", classification_report(y_test, y_pred))
```

In this code:

- We use **TfidfVectorizer** to convert text into numerical features (TF-IDF).

- We split the data into training and test sets using train_test_split.
- We train the model using **Multinomial Naive Bayes** (which is often effective for text classification).
- We evaluate the model's accuracy and generate a classification report that includes precision, recall, and F1-score.

Comparing Various Machine Learning Algorithms for Intent Classification

Different machine learning algorithms can perform differently depending on the nature of your data. Below, we will compare some popular algorithms for intent classification.

1. **Logistic Regression**: Logistic Regression is a widely-used linear classifier. It's simple, interpretable, and performs well on text classification tasks with a large number of features.

python

```
from sklearn.linear_model import LogisticRegression

# Train the Logistic Regression model
lr_model = LogisticRegression(max_iter=200)
lr_model.fit(X_train, y_train)

# Evaluate the model
y_pred_lr = lr_model.predict(X_test)
```

```
print("Logistic    Regression    Accuracy:",    accuracy_score(y_test,
y_pred_lr))
print("Classification    Report    for    Logistic    Regression:\n",
classification_report(y_test, y_pred_lr))
```

2. **Naive Bayes**: Naive Bayes classifiers work well when features are independent. It is especially good with large feature sets and performs well for tasks like spam filtering and text classification.

python

```
from sklearn.naive_bayes import MultinomialNB

# Train the Naive Bayes model
nb_model = MultinomialNB()
nb_model.fit(X_train, y_train)

# Evaluate the model
y_pred_nb = nb_model.predict(X_test)
print("Naive Bayes Accuracy:", accuracy_score(y_test, y_pred_nb))
print("Classification    Report    for    Naive    Bayes:\n",
classification_report(y_test, y_pred_nb))
```

3. **Support Vector Machine (SVM)**: SVM is a powerful classifier that works well on high-dimensional datasets. It tries to find the hyperplane that maximizes the margin between classes.

python

```python
from sklearn.svm import SVC

# Train the SVM model
svm_model = SVC(kernel='linear')
svm_model.fit(X_train, y_train)

# Evaluate the model
y_pred_svm = svm_model.predict(X_test)
print("SVM Accuracy:", accuracy_score(y_test, y_pred_svm))
print("Classification Report for SVM:\n", classification_report(y_test, y_pred_svm))
```

4. **Random Forest**: Random Forest is an ensemble method that uses multiple decision trees to improve performance. It is a good choice for large datasets and can handle complex relationships between features.

python

```python
from sklearn.ensemble import RandomForestClassifier

# Train the Random Forest model
rf_model = RandomForestClassifier(n_estimators=100)
rf_model.fit(X_train, y_train)

# Evaluate the model
y_pred_rf = rf_model.predict(X_test)
print("Random Forest Accuracy:", accuracy_score(y_test, y_pred_rf))
```

```
print("Classification     Report     for     Random     Forest:\n",
classification_report(y_test, y_pred_rf))
```

Evaluating Model Performance

To evaluate the performance of your intent classification model, we can use the following metrics:

1. **Accuracy**: The proportion of correct predictions out of all predictions.
   - Formula: Accuracy = (True Positives + True Negatives) / Total Predictions
2. **Precision**: The proportion of true positive predictions out of all positive predictions.
   - Formula: Precision = True Positives / (True Positives + False Positives)
3. **Recall (Sensitivity)**: The proportion of true positive predictions out of all actual positives.
   - Formula: Recall = True Positives / (True Positives + False Negatives)
4. **F1 Score**: The harmonic mean of precision and recall, balancing both metrics.
   - Formula: F1 Score = 2 * (Precision * Recall) / (Precision + Recall)

You can evaluate these metrics using **classification_report** from scikit-learn, which provides a detailed report for each class.

python

```
from sklearn.metrics import classification_report

# Generate classification report
print(classification_report(y_test, y_pred))
```

This function provides precision, recall, F1-score, and support (the number of occurrences for each class) for each class in the classification task.

In this chapter, we learned how to implement **intent classification** for chatbots using machine learning. We explored several algorithms, including **Logistic Regression**, **Naive Bayes**, **SVM**, and **Random Forest**, and compared their performance on a simple dataset. We also discussed how to evaluate the performance of the model using metrics like accuracy, precision, recall, and F1-score.

By selecting the best-performing model, you can enhance your chatbot's ability to classify user queries into relevant intents, improving the overall user experience.

Chapter 12: Handling User Input and Responses

In this chapter, we will explore how to effectively **capture and process user input dynamically**, design **chatbot responses**, and **personalize responses using context** to make chatbot interactions more natural and engaging. These skills are fundamental for building a responsive and user-friendly chatbot that can handle various scenarios.

Capturing and Processing User Input Dynamically

Capturing user input and processing it dynamically is one of the first steps in building a chatbot. The user's message is often unstructured and can come in many different forms, so it's essential for the chatbot to process and understand the input effectively.

1. **Capturing User Input**: In Python, capturing user input can be done using the input() function. This allows the chatbot to wait for user input and store the result for further processing.

   Example:

   python

   ```
   user_input = input("You: ")  # Capture user input
   ```

2. **Processing User Input**: Once the input is captured, it needs to be processed to identify intent, extract key information, and decide on the appropriate response. Processing involves steps like:

   o **Cleaning the text** (e.g., removing unnecessary punctuation, converting to lowercase)

   o **Tokenization** (splitting the text into smaller units like words or phrases)

   o **Intent classification** (identifying the user's goal, e.g., greeting, query about weather)

   o **Entity extraction** (extracting specific details, like dates or locations)

For example, if the user asks, "What is the weather in Paris?", the chatbot should:

   o Recognize the intent as a **weather query**.

   o Extract **"Paris"** as the **location**.

Processing Flow Example:

python

```
def process_input(user_input):
    # Clean and tokenize input (simplified)
    processed_input = user_input.lower().strip()
    return processed_input
```

```
user_input = input("You: ")
processed_input = process_input(user_input)
print(f"Processed Input: {processed_input}")
```

3. **Handling User Input Dynamically**: The chatbot should respond dynamically based on different inputs. For instance, a chatbot can handle greetings differently than it handles queries about the weather. Here's a simple dynamic response system:

Example:

python

```
def respond_to_input(processed_input):
    if "hello" in processed_input or "hi" in processed_input:
        return "Hello! How can I assist you today?"
    elif "weather" in processed_input:
        return "Sure! I can help you with the weather. Where would you
like to know the weather for?"
    else:
        return "Sorry, I didn't quite understand that. Can you rephrase?"

response = respond_to_input(processed_input)
print(f"Bot: {response}")
```

In this simple flow:

- The chatbot checks if the user's message contains certain keywords (e.g., "hello" or "weather").

- It responds dynamically based on the presence of these keywords.

Designing Chatbot Responses

Designing chatbot responses is crucial for creating a positive user experience. The responses should be relevant, informative, and conversational.

1. **Response Format**: Chatbot responses should be designed based on the intent of the user input. The chatbot can offer several types of responses:
   - **Informational Responses**: These provide factual information, such as weather updates or product details.
   - **Confirmation Responses**: These acknowledge user actions or inputs (e.g., confirming an order or appointment).
   - **Clarification Responses**: If the chatbot is uncertain about the user's input, it can ask follow-up questions or offer clarification.
2. **Handling Simple Queries**: For simple, straightforward queries, the chatbot should return a direct, informative response.

   Example:

   python

```
def respond_to_weather_query(location):
    return f"The weather in {location} is sunny and 75°F today."

location = "Paris"
response = respond_to_weather_query(location)
print(f"Bot: {response}")
```

3. **Personalized Responses**: To enhance user experience, chatbots should **personalize responses** based on context or user-specific data, such as their name, preferences, or previous interactions.

   Example (Simple Personalization):

   python

```
def personalized_response(user_name):
    return f"Hello {user_name}, how can I assist you today?"

user_name = "Alice"
response = personalized_response(user_name)
print(f"Bot: {response}")
```

4. **Contextual Responses**: In more sophisticated chatbot designs, responses can be context-sensitive. For example, the chatbot can remember previous interactions and provide responses based on that context.

   Example:

python

```
def contextual_response(user_input, context):
    if "book" in user_input and context.get('action') == "booking_flight":
        return "I see you're booking a flight. Where would you like to go?"
    elif "cancel" in user_input and context.get('action') == "booking_flight":
        return "You are trying to cancel your flight booking. Would you like to proceed?"
    else:
        return "I didn't quite catch that. Can you clarify?"

# Assuming context has been set earlier in the conversation
context = {'action': 'booking_flight'}
user_input = "cancel my flight"
response = contextual_response(user_input, context)
print(f'Bot: {response}")
```

In this case, the chatbot recognizes that the user is in the process of booking a flight and offers responses based on that context.

Personalizing Responses Using Context

Context plays a crucial role in personalizing chatbot responses and making them more relevant to the user's needs. By maintaining context across interactions, the chatbot can provide more intelligent and tailored conversations.

1. **Storing Context**: The context can include information like:
    o   **User details** (e.g., name, preferences)

- ○ **Conversation history** (e.g., what the user has asked previously)

- ○ **Session data** (e.g., items added to a cart, ongoing bookings)

Example of storing and using context:

python

```
def update_context(user_input, context):
    if "book a flight" in user_input:
        context['action'] = 'booking_flight'
        return "What is your destination?"
    elif "name" in user_input:
        context['user_name'] = user_input.split(" ")[-1]
        return f"Hello {context['user_name']}! How can I assist you today?"
    else:
        return "I didn't understand that."

# Initialize empty context
context = {}

# Simulate conversation flow
user_input = "book a flight"
response = update_context(user_input, context)
print(f"Bot: {response}")

user_input = "John"
response = update_context(user_input, context)
```

```
print(f"Bot: {response}")
```

In this example, the chatbot updates the context with the action being taken (e.g., booking a flight) and stores the user's name. This allows the chatbot to respond more appropriately to future queries.

2. **Session Management**: To maintain a consistent conversation, it's important for the chatbot to keep track of **session state**. For instance, if a user is in the process of booking a flight, the chatbot should continue asking questions related to the flight (e.g., destination, date, etc.) until the booking is complete.

   Example of session management:

   python

```
def handle_booking_session(user_input, session):
    if session.get('action') == 'booking_flight':
        if 'destination' not in session:
            session['destination'] = user_input
            return "Got it! When would you like to fly?"
        elif 'date' not in session:
            session['date'] = user_input
            return f"Your flight to {session['destination']} is booked for
{session['date']}."
    else:
        return "I don't know how to help with that right now."


# Simulating the booking process
```

```
session = {'action': 'booking_flight'}
user_input = "Paris"
print(handle_booking_session(user_input, session))

user_input = "March 10th"
print(handle_booking_session(user_input, session))
```

In this example, the chatbot uses the session to track the user's progress in booking a flight and provides contextually relevant responses.

In this chapter, we've covered how to:

- **Capture and process user input dynamically** using functions like input().

- **Design chatbot responses** that are informative, engaging, and relevant.

- **Personalize responses** using context, allowing the chatbot to adapt to different situations and remember past interactions.

By incorporating context, user-specific data, and dynamic response generation, chatbots can provide a more natural and personalized experience, making interactions smoother and more intuitive.

Chapter 13: Building a Retrieval-Based Chatbot

In this chapter, we will discuss how to build a **retrieval-based chatbot**, which is a type of chatbot that selects an appropriate response from a predefined set of responses based on the user's input. These chatbots do not generate responses from scratch, but instead retrieve the most relevant response from a knowledge base or a collection of responses. We will also explore how to enhance the chatbot with better response matching techniques to make it more effective.

What is a Retrieval-Based Chatbot?

A **retrieval-based chatbot** is a type of conversational AI that works by matching the user's query with the most relevant response from a set of predefined responses or a knowledge base. This type of chatbot doesn't generate responses but retrieves and returns the most suitable one based on the input it receives. The focus is on **matching patterns** in the user input with predefined patterns associated with responses.

Key Characteristics of a Retrieval-Based Chatbot:

1. **Predefined Responses**: The bot doesn't generate text; it selects the best response from a database of predefined responses.

2. **Pattern Matching**: The bot typically uses algorithms to find patterns in the user's input and matches it to predefined queries or responses.

3. **Intent Recognition**: The chatbot often relies on **intent classification** (as discussed in earlier chapters) to understand the user's query and find the most relevant response.

4. **Simple and Fast**: These chatbots are typically quicker and easier to deploy than generative chatbots because they do not require complex language generation capabilities.

Implementing a Simple Retrieval-Based Chatbot

To implement a simple retrieval-based chatbot, we need:

1. A set of predefined responses.
2. A mechanism to process and match the user's input to these responses.

Let's build a simple retrieval-based chatbot where we manually define intents and their corresponding responses.

1. **Define Intents and Responses**: We will create a small set of intents, such as "greeting", "goodbye", and "weather inquiry", along with corresponding responses.

2. **Match User Input to Intents**: We will use simple keyword matching or regular expressions to identify the intent of the user's input.

3. **Select and Return the Best Response**: Once the intent is identified, the bot will retrieve the most appropriate response from the predefined responses.

Example Code:

python

```python
import re

# Define intents and responses
intents = {
    "greeting": ["Hello!", "Hi there!", "Greetings!", "Good to see you!"],
    "goodbye": ["Goodbye!", "See you later!", "Have a nice day!", "Take care!"],
    "weather": ["The weather is sunny.", "It looks like rain today.", "It's cloudy today.", "Expect a clear sky."]
}

# Function to match input to intents
def match_intent(user_input):
    user_input = user_input.lower()
    if re.search(r"(hello|hi|hey)", user_input):
        return "greeting"
    elif re.search(r"(bye|goodbye|see you)", user_input):
        return "goodbye"
    elif re.search(r"(weather|forecast|temperature)", user_input):
        return "weather"
    else:
        return None
```

```python
# Function to get response based on intent
def get_response(intent):
    if intent and intent in intents:
        return intents[intent][0]  # For simplicity, return the first response
    else:
        return "Sorry, I didn't understand that."


# Example interaction
user_input = input("You: ")
intent = match_intent(user_input)
response = get_response(intent)
print(f"Bot: {response}")
```

Explanation:

- **Intents**: We define a simple dictionary of intents with corresponding responses.
- **Pattern Matching**: We use regular expressions (via re.search()) to match user input to specific patterns (e.g., greetings or weather inquiries).
- **Response Retrieval**: Once an intent is identified, the bot returns a predefined response associated with that intent.

Sample interaction:

vbnet

You: What's the weather like today?
Bot: The weather is sunny.

Enhancing the Chatbot with Better Response Matching

While the above chatbot works for basic input, it can be enhanced for better response matching by incorporating techniques such as:

1. **Cosine Similarity**: Measures the similarity between two text vectors and returns the most similar response.

2. **TF-IDF (Term Frequency-Inverse Document Frequency)**: Used to convert user input into numerical vectors, improving how we match it to predefined responses.

3. **Keyword Extraction**: Extracts important keywords from the user input to match with relevant responses more effectively.

Here's how to enhance the retrieval-based chatbot by incorporating **TF-IDF** and **Cosine Similarity** for more sophisticated matching.

Step 1: Use TF-IDF for Feature Extraction

We will use **TF-IDF** to convert both the user input and predefined responses into vectors and then compute the cosine similarity between them.

Example Code:

python

```
from sklearn.feature_extraction.text import TfidfVectorizer
from sklearn.metrics.pairwise import cosine_similarity

# Define predefined responses
responses = [
```

```
    "Hello, how can I assist you today?",
    "Goodbye! Take care.",
    "The weather is sunny and warm today.",
    "I'm sorry, I didn't understand your request."
]


# Function to get the best response based on input
def get_best_response(user_input, responses):
    vectorizer = TfidfVectorizer(stop_words="english")
    all_texts = responses + [user_input]

    # Transform both user input and predefined responses into vectors
    tfidf_matrix = vectorizer.fit_transform(all_texts)

    # Compute cosine similarity between the input and all predefined responses
    cosine_similarities = cosine_similarity(tfidf_matrix[-1], tfidf_matrix[:-1])

    # Get the index of the most similar response
    best_match_idx = cosine_similarities.argmax()
    return responses[best_match_idx]

# Example interaction
user_input = input("You: ")
response = get_best_response(user_input, responses)
print(f"Bot: {response}")
```

Explanation:

1. **TF-IDF Vectorization**: The TfidfVectorizer converts the user input and predefined responses into numerical vectors based on term frequency and inverse document frequency.

2. **Cosine Similarity**: The cosine_similarity function calculates how similar the user input is to each of the predefined responses.

3. **Best Match**: The chatbot returns the response with the highest similarity score.

Sample interaction:

vbnet

You: What's the weather today?
Bot: The weather is sunny and warm today.

Step 2: Handling Context for Enhanced Matching

To further enhance the chatbot, you can incorporate **context** into the response matching. For instance, if the user asks a follow-up question related to weather, the chatbot should remember the previous context and provide a more relevant answer.

Here's an enhancement to store and use context in the chatbot:

Example Code with Context:

python

```python
context = {}

def update_context(user_input):
    if "weather" in user_input:
        context["last_intent"] = "weather"
```

```
        return "What location would you like the weather for?"
    elif "location" in user_input:
        context["location"] = user_input
        return f"The weather in {user_input} is sunny and warm today."
    else:
        return "Sorry, I didn't understand that."

# Example interaction with context
user_input = input("You: ")
response = update_context(user_input)
print(f"Bot: {response}")


user_input = input("You: ")
response = update_context(user_input)
print(f"Bot: {response}")
```

Explanation:

- The chatbot remembers the **last intent** and stores **location** context based on the user's input. This allows it to provide more personalized and relevant responses based on previous interactions.

Sample interaction with context:

vbnet

You: What's the weather like?
Bot: What location would you like the weather for?
You: Paris
Bot: The weather in Paris is sunny and warm today.

In this chapter, we explored **retrieval-based chatbots**, which select the most appropriate response from a predefined set of responses based on the user's input. We implemented a simple retrieval-based chatbot and enhanced it with better **response matching** using **TF-IDF** and **cosine similarity**. Additionally, we discussed how to incorporate **context** to make the chatbot's responses more relevant and personalized.

By using these techniques, your chatbot can provide more dynamic and intelligent interactions, improving user satisfaction and engagement.

Chapter 14: Building a Generative Chatbot

In this chapter, we will explore **generative chatbots**, which differ from retrieval-based chatbots in that they **generate** responses dynamically instead of selecting them from a predefined set. We will discuss the basics of generative chatbots, introduce **sequence-to-sequence models** (which form the backbone of many generative chatbots), and show how to train a generative chatbot using Python.

Introduction to Generative Chatbots

Generative chatbots are designed to **generate** responses based on the input they receive. Unlike retrieval-based chatbots, which rely on a fixed set of responses, generative chatbots produce responses from scratch, allowing for more flexible and dynamic interactions. This ability makes generative chatbots more capable of handling diverse user queries, even those they have not been explicitly trained for.

Key Characteristics of Generative Chatbots:

1. **Response Generation**: They generate responses dynamically, rather than retrieving them from a database.
2. **Understanding Context**: They often maintain the conversation context, allowing for more natural and coherent dialogues.

3. **Flexibility**: They can handle any type of user input as long as they have been trained on sufficient data.

Generative chatbots typically use **sequence-to-sequence (Seq2Seq)** models, which are a type of deep learning architecture designed to map an input sequence (e.g., a user query) to an output sequence (e.g., the bot's response). These models are often used in applications like machine translation, text summarization, and chatbot development.

Using Sequence-to-Sequence Models

Sequence-to-sequence (Seq2Seq) models are built using two main components:

1. **Encoder**: This part of the model processes the input sequence (user's message) and compresses the information into a fixed-length vector (also known as the context or thought vector).
2. **Decoder**: The decoder takes this context vector and generates the output sequence (the chatbot's response).

Architecture of Seq2Seq Models:

- The **encoder** and **decoder** are typically implemented using Recurrent Neural Networks (RNNs), Long Short-Term Memory (LSTM), or Gated Recurrent Units (GRUs).

- The **attention mechanism** can also be added to allow the model to focus on different parts of the input sequence when generating each word in the output.

Seq2Seq models have been used successfully for various tasks, including:

- **Machine Translation**: Translating one language to another.
- **Text Summarization**: Generating a summary of a long text.
- **Conversational AI**: Generating chatbot responses.

Training a Generative Chatbot with Python

Let's walk through how you can train a simple generative chatbot using Python. For simplicity, we'll use a sequence-to-sequence model with LSTM units and train it on a small dataset.

Step 1: Prepare the Dataset

For training a generative chatbot, you'll need pairs of input-output sentences (e.g., "How are you?" -> "I'm good, thank you!"). You can use datasets like **Cornell Movie Dialogues**, **Persona-Chat**, or any dataset that contains conversational pairs.

For this example, let's assume we have a small dataset of paired sentences like the following:

Input	Output
"Hello!"	"Hi, how can I help you?"
"How are you?"	"I'm good, thank you!"
"What is your name?"	"I'm a chatbot!"
"Goodbye!"	"See you later!"

Step 2: Preprocess the Text Data

We need to preprocess the input and output text before feeding it into the model:

- **Tokenization**: Break the text into individual words or tokens.
- **Padding**: Ensure that all sequences are of the same length.
- **Vocabulary Creation**: Create a vocabulary of all the unique words in the dataset.

We will use **Keras** and **TensorFlow** for building and training the model. First, install the required libraries:

bash

```
pip install tensorflow keras
```

Here is how to preprocess the dataset:

python

```python
import numpy as np
from tensorflow.keras.preprocessing.text import Tokenizer
from tensorflow.keras.preprocessing.sequence import pad_sequences

# Example dataset
input_texts = ["Hello!", "How are you?", "What is your name?", "Goodbye!"]
output_texts = ["Hi, how can I help you?", "I'm good, thank you!", "I'm a chatbot!", "See you later!"]

# Tokenize input and output texts
input_tokenizer = Tokenizer()
input_tokenizer.fit_on_texts(input_texts)
input_sequences = input_tokenizer.texts_to_sequences(input_texts)

output_tokenizer = Tokenizer()
output_tokenizer.fit_on_texts(output_texts)
output_sequences = output_tokenizer.texts_to_sequences(output_texts)

# Pad the sequences to have equal length
max_input_len = max([len(seq) for seq in input_sequences])
max_output_len = max([len(seq) for seq in output_sequences])

X = pad_sequences(input_sequences, maxlen=max_input_len, padding='post')
y = pad_sequences(output_sequences, maxlen=max_output_len, padding='post')

# Vocabulary size
input_vocab_size = len(input_tokenizer.word_index) + 1
output_vocab_size = len(output_tokenizer.word_index) + 1

print(X)
```

print(y)

Step 3: Build the Seq2Seq Model

We will now build a sequence-to-sequence model using **LSTM layers** in Keras.

python

```python
from tensorflow.keras.models import Model
from tensorflow.keras.layers import Input, LSTM, Embedding, Dense

# Define the encoder
encoder_inputs = Input(shape=(max_input_len,))
encoder_embedding = Embedding(input_dim=input_vocab_size, output_dim=256)(encoder_inputs)
encoder_lstm = LSTM(256, return_state=True)
encoder_outputs, state_h, state_c = encoder_lstm(encoder_embedding)

# Define the decoder
decoder_inputs = Input(shape=(max_output_len,))
decoder_embedding = Embedding(input_dim=output_vocab_size, output_dim=256)(decoder_inputs)
decoder_lstm = LSTM(256, return_sequences=True)(decoder_embedding, initial_state=[state_h, state_c])
decoder_dense = Dense(output_vocab_size, activation='softmax')
decoder_outputs = decoder_dense(decoder_lstm)

# Create and compile the model
model = Model([encoder_inputs, decoder_inputs], decoder_outputs)
model.compile(optimizer='adam', loss='sparse_categorical_crossentropy', metrics=['accuracy'])
```

```
# Train the model
model.fit([X, y], np.expand_dims(y, -1), epochs=50, batch_size=32)
```

Here, we:

- **Encoder**: An embedding layer followed by an LSTM to process the input sequence and output its final hidden and cell states.
- **Decoder**: An embedding layer followed by an LSTM that takes the encoder's hidden states as initial states and generates the output sequence.
- **Dense Layer**: A softmax output layer that predicts the next word in the sequence.

Step 4: Making Predictions with the Model

Once the model is trained, we can use it to generate responses for new input queries. The basic idea is:

1. Encode the user's input to obtain the context vector (hidden and cell states).
2. Use the context vector to generate a response one word at a time, feeding the output of the decoder back into the model until the end of the sequence is reached.

Example Code for Making Predictions:

python

```python
def predict_response(input_text):
    # Tokenize and pad the input text
    input_sequence = input_tokenizer.texts_to_sequences([input_text])
    input_sequence = pad_sequences(input_sequence, maxlen=max_input_len,
padding='post')

    # Encode the input sequence
    states_value = encoder_lstm.predict(input_sequence)

    # Generate the response sequence
    target_sequence = np.zeros((1, max_output_len))
    target_sequence[0, 0] = output_tokenizer.word_index['start']  # Add start token

    response = []
    for i in range(1, max_output_len):
        output_tokens = decoder_dense.predict([target_sequence] + states_value)
        predicted_token_index = np.argmax(output_tokens[0, i-1])
        predicted_token = output_tokenizer.index_word[predicted_token_index]

        # Stop when we reach the end token
        if predicted_token == 'end':
            break

        response.append(predicted_token)

        # Update the target sequence
        target_sequence[0, i] = predicted_token_index
        states_value = [states_value[0], states_value[1]]

    return ' '.join(response)
```

```
# Test the chatbot with a sample input
user_input = "Hello!"
response = predict_response(user_input)
print(f"Chatbot: {response}")
```

Step 5: Improving the Generative Chatbot

To improve the generative chatbot:

1. **Use a Larger Dataset**: The quality of the chatbot improves with a larger, more diverse dataset.

2. **Implement Attention Mechanisms**: Attention mechanisms allow the model to focus on specific parts of the input sequence when generating the output.

3. **Fine-tune Hyperparameters**: Experiment with different values for the number of layers, units in each layer, learning rate, etc., to improve model performance.

4. **Use Pretrained Models**: You can use pretrained models such as GPT-2 or GPT-3 (for large-scale conversational AI) to significantly improve the performance.

In this chapter, we built a **generative chatbot** using a **sequence-to-sequence model**. We walked through the process of preparing the dataset, building the Seq2Seq model, and generating responses. Generative models are powerful because they can produce novel, dynamic responses, making them ideal for complex chatbot interactions.

Chapter 15: Integrating NLP with Deep Learning Models

In this chapter, we will explore how **deep learning** techniques can be integrated with **Natural Language Processing (NLP)** to solve complex NLP tasks. We will cover how deep learning is revolutionizing NLP, discuss how it is used in more sophisticated NLP tasks, and provide examples of how to implement deep learning models using **TensorFlow** and **PyTorch**.

Overview of Deep Learning Techniques in NLP

Deep learning techniques, particularly **neural networks**, have significantly improved the performance of NLP tasks. These techniques are well-suited for handling the complexity and high dimensionality of natural language. Below are some key deep learning techniques commonly used in NLP:

1. **Word Embeddings**: Word embeddings, such as **Word2Vec**, **GloVe**, and **FastText**, are dense vector representations of words. They allow models to capture semantic meanings and relationships between words. Deep learning models like **Recurrent Neural Networks (RNNs)**, **Long Short-Term Memory networks (LSTMs)**, and **Transformers** utilize word embeddings as input to understand the structure and meaning of text.

2. **Recurrent Neural Networks (RNNs)**: RNNs are neural networks designed to process sequences of data, such as text. They have an internal state that helps them remember information about previous words, making them suitable for tasks like language modeling, text generation, and machine translation.

3. **Long Short-Term Memory (LSTM)**: LSTMs are a type of RNN that mitigates the vanishing gradient problem, allowing them to learn long-term dependencies. They are used in tasks that require understanding the context over long sequences, such as in chatbots and speech recognition.

4. **Transformers**: Transformers are a more recent innovation in deep learning for NLP. Unlike RNNs, transformers process entire sequences of text in parallel rather than one word at a time, enabling much faster training. They form the backbone of state-of-the-art models like **BERT, GPT**, and **T5**.

5. **Attention Mechanism**: The attention mechanism allows a model to focus on important parts of the input sequence while generating each word in the output sequence. This is crucial in tasks like machine translation and text summarization.

6. **Pretrained Models**: Models such as **BERT** (Bidirectional Encoder Representations from Transformers) and **GPT** (Generative Pretrained Transformer) are trained on massive

amounts of text data and can be fine-tuned for a variety of downstream NLP tasks like question answering, text classification, and more.

Using Deep Learning for More Complex NLP Tasks

Deep learning models are capable of handling a wide range of NLP tasks that go beyond traditional methods. Some of these tasks include:

1. **Text Classification**: Classifying text into categories (e.g., spam detection, sentiment analysis). Deep learning models can learn the underlying features of the text without the need for extensive feature engineering.

2. **Named Entity Recognition (NER)**: Identifying entities such as names, organizations, locations, and dates in text. Deep learning models like LSTMs and Transformers are commonly used for NER tasks.

3. **Question Answering**: Given a passage of text, deep learning models can be trained to extract relevant answers to questions. This is the basis for models like **BERT**.

4. **Machine Translation**: Automatically translating text from one language to another. Transformers and Seq2Seq models with attention mechanisms have revolutionized this area.

5. **Text Generation**: Generating human-like text, such as chat responses or story generation. Generative models like **GPT-**

2 and **GPT-3** excel in this task by predicting the next word in a sequence.

6. **Text Summarization**: Generating a concise summary of a longer document. Deep learning-based models use both extractive and abstractive summarization techniques.

Implementing Deep Learning Models with TensorFlow and PyTorch

Now let's dive into **TensorFlow** and **PyTorch**, two of the most popular deep learning frameworks for implementing NLP models.

Implementing Deep Learning Models with TensorFlow

TensorFlow is an open-source machine learning framework developed by Google, widely used for training deep learning models. It is particularly popular for deploying models at scale.

Step 1: Install TensorFlow

bash

```
pip install tensorflow
```

Step 2: Implementing a Simple Text Classification Model

We'll create a simple deep learning model using **LSTM** for text classification.

python

```
import tensorflow as tf
```

```
from tensorflow.keras.preprocessing.text import Tokenizer
from tensorflow.keras.preprocessing.sequence import pad_sequences
from tensorflow.keras.models import Sequential
from tensorflow.keras.layers import Embedding, LSTM, Dense


# Example dataset (sentences and corresponding labels)
texts = ["I love programming", "I hate bugs", "Python is great", "I dislike errors"]
labels = [1, 0, 1, 0]  # 1 = positive, 0 = negative


# Step 1: Tokenize the text
tokenizer = Tokenizer(num_words=1000, oov_token="<OOV>")
tokenizer.fit_on_texts(texts)
sequences = tokenizer.texts_to_sequences(texts)
X = pad_sequences(sequences, padding='post')


# Step 2: Define the model
model = Sequential()
model.add(Embedding(input_dim=1000,                        output_dim=64,
input_length=X.shape[1]))
model.add(LSTM(64))
model.add(Dense(1, activation='sigmoid'))


# Step 3: Compile and train the model
model.compile(optimizer='adam',                loss='binary_crossentropy',
metrics=['accuracy'])
model.fit(X, labels, epochs=10)


# Step 4: Make predictions
test_texts = ["I enjoy coding", "I can't stand bugs"]
test_sequences = tokenizer.texts_to_sequences(test_texts)
```

```
test_X = pad_sequences(test_sequences, padding='post', maxlen=X.shape[1])
predictions = model.predict(test_X)
print(predictions)
```

Explanation:

- **Tokenizer**: Tokenizes the input text and converts it into sequences of integers.
- **LSTM**: A Long Short-Term Memory layer to learn from the sequential data.
- **Dense Layer**: A fully connected layer for output (binary classification).
- We use the **binary crossentropy** loss function since this is a binary classification problem (positive vs. negative sentiment).

Implementing Deep Learning Models with PyTorch

PyTorch is another powerful deep learning framework developed by Facebook. It's known for its dynamic computation graph and ease of use in research.

Step 1: Install PyTorch

bash

```
pip install torch torchvision
```

Step 2: Implementing a Simple Text Classification Model with LSTM

python

```
import torch
import torch.nn as nn
from torch.utils.data import DataLoader, TensorDataset

# Example dataset (sentences and corresponding labels)
texts = ["I love programming", "I hate bugs", "Python is great", "I dislike errors"]
labels = torch.tensor([1, 0, 1, 0])  # 1 = positive, 0 = negative

# Tokenize the text (same as in TensorFlow example, just for demonstration)
# For simplicity, we use pre-tokenized integers (in a real-world scenario, you'd
tokenize text similarly as in TensorFlow)
sequences = [[1, 2, 3], [4, 5], [6, 7, 8], [9, 10]]  # Example tokenized sentences
X = torch.tensor(sequences)
max_len = max(len(seq) for seq in sequences)
X = torch.nn.functional.pad(X, (0, max_len - X.shape[1]))

# Step 1: Define the model
class LSTMModel(nn.Module):
    def __init__(self, input_dim, embedding_dim, hidden_dim, output_dim):
        super(LSTMModel, self).__init__()
        self.embedding = nn.Embedding(input_dim, embedding_dim)
        self.lstm = nn.LSTM(embedding_dim, hidden_dim)
        self.fc = nn.Linear(hidden_dim, output_dim)

    def forward(self, x):
        embedded = self.embedding(x)
        lstm_out, (h_n, c_n) = self.lstm(embedded)
        out = self.fc(h_n[-1])
        return out
```

```python
# Step 2: Instantiate and train the model
model = LSTMModel(input_dim=1000, embedding_dim=64, hidden_dim=64,
output_dim=1)
loss_fn = nn.BCEWithLogitsLoss()
optimizer = torch.optim.Adam(model.parameters(), lr=0.001)


# Step 3: Prepare the data and train the model
dataset = TensorDataset(X, labels)
loader = DataLoader(dataset, batch_size=2, shuffle=True)


for epoch in range(10):
    for batch in loader:
        inputs, target = batch
        optimizer.zero_grad()
        output = model(inputs)
        loss = loss_fn(output.squeeze(), target.float())
        loss.backward()
        optimizer.step()


# Step 4: Make predictions
test_texts = torch.tensor([[1, 2, 3], [4, 5, 6]])
predictions = model(test_texts)
print(predictions)
```

Explanation:

- **Embedding Layer**: Transforms tokenized text into dense vectors.
- **LSTM Layer**: Processes the sequential data.

- **Fully Connected Layer**: Outputs a classification score, which we convert to binary (positive/negative).

In this chapter, we integrated **deep learning** models with **Natural Language Processing** tasks. We introduced key techniques such as **RNNs**, **LSTMs**, and **Transformers**, and discussed how they are used in complex NLP tasks like text classification, question answering, and text generation. We also provided examples of how to implement deep learning models using **TensorFlow** and **PyTorch**, two of the most widely used deep learning frameworks.

By using deep learning models, we can take NLP tasks to the next level, achieving more accurate and flexible solutions. Would you like to dive deeper into any specific deep learning technique or explore more complex tasks like fine-tuning pre-trained models such as BERT or GPT-3?

Chapter 16: Building a Sentiment Analysis Chatbot

In this chapter, we will explore **sentiment analysis**, an important task in Natural Language Processing (NLP) that can be used to build smarter chatbots. We will learn what sentiment analysis is, how to build a sentiment analysis model for a chatbot, and explore various **use cases** of sentiment analysis in chatbot applications.

What is Sentiment Analysis?

Sentiment analysis is the process of determining the emotional tone or sentiment expressed in a piece of text. The goal is to classify the sentiment of a text as positive, negative, or neutral (or even more specific categories, such as "angry," "happy," "sad," etc.).

Sentiment analysis can be applied to:

- **Reviews and Feedback**: Analyzing customer feedback to understand if users are happy with a product or service.
- **Social Media Monitoring**: Assessing the public sentiment around a brand, topic, or event.
- **Customer Support**: Understanding whether a customer is satisfied, frustrated, or neutral during interactions.

Key Steps in Sentiment Analysis:

1. **Preprocessing**: Clean and tokenize the text, handle stop words, lemmatization, etc.

2. **Feature Extraction**: Convert text into a numerical representation (e.g., TF-IDF, word embeddings).

3. **Model Training**: Train a machine learning or deep learning model to classify sentiment.

4. **Prediction**: Use the trained model to classify new user inputs as positive, negative, or neutral.

Building a Sentiment Analysis Model for Your Chatbot

To build a sentiment analysis model for your chatbot, we need to:

1. **Prepare the dataset**: We need a labeled dataset with text and corresponding sentiment labels (e.g., "positive," "negative," "neutral").

2. **Preprocess the text**: This involves steps like tokenization, stopword removal, and text normalization.

3. **Train a model**: We will use a machine learning model (e.g., Logistic Regression, Naive Bayes) or a deep learning model (e.g., LSTM, BERT).

4. **Integrate the model into the chatbot**: Once the model is trained, we can integrate it into the chatbot to analyze the sentiment of user inputs dynamically.

Step 1: Prepare the Dataset

For sentiment analysis, we can use publicly available datasets such as **IMDb Movie Reviews**, **Sentiment140**, or **Twitter Sentiment Analysis** datasets. These datasets typically contain labeled sentences with sentiments (e.g., "positive," "negative").

Here's an example of a simple dataset:

Text	Sentiment
"I love this product!"	Positive
"This is terrible, I hate it."	Negative
"It's okay, not great, not bad."	Neutral

Step 2: Preprocess the Text Data

We need to preprocess the text data before feeding it into the sentiment analysis model. Preprocessing involves:

- **Tokenization**: Splitting the text into words or tokens.
- **Stopword Removal**: Removing common words that don't contribute much to sentiment analysis (e.g., "is", "the").
- **Lemmatization/Stemming**: Reducing words to their base form (e.g., "running" becomes "run").

We can use **nltk** or **spaCy** to handle this preprocessing. Here's an example using nltk:

python

```python
import nltk
from nltk.tokenize import word_tokenize
from nltk.corpus import stopwords
from nltk.stem import WordNetLemmatizer

# Download necessary nltk resources
nltk.download('punkt')
nltk.download('stopwords')
nltk.download('wordnet')

# Initialize lemmatizer and stopwords list
lemmatizer = WordNetLemmatizer()
stop_words = set(stopwords.words('english'))

# Preprocessing function
def preprocess_text(text):
    words = word_tokenize(text.lower())  # Convert to lowercase and tokenize
    return [lemmatizer.lemmatize(word) for word in words if word not in stop_words]

# Example preprocessing
text = "I love this product!"
preprocessed_text = preprocess_text(text)
print(preprocessed_text)
```

Step 3: Train a Sentiment Analysis Model

Once the data is preprocessed, we can proceed with training a sentiment analysis model. For simplicity, let's use a **Naive Bayes**

classifier with **TF-IDF** features, which is effective for many text classification tasks.

Example Code for Model Training:

python

```
from sklearn.feature_extraction.text import TfidfVectorizer
from sklearn.naive_bayes import MultinomialNB
from sklearn.model_selection import train_test_split
from sklearn.metrics import accuracy_score, classification_report

# Example dataset
texts = ["I love this product!", "This is terrible, I hate it.", "It's okay, not great, not bad."]
labels = ['Positive', 'Negative', 'Neutral']  # Sentiments

# Step 1: Preprocess the dataset
texts_preprocessed = [preprocess_text(text) for text in texts]
texts_preprocessed = [' '.join(text) for text in texts_preprocessed]

# Step 2: Convert texts to TF-IDF features
vectorizer = TfidfVectorizer()
X = vectorizer.fit_transform(texts_preprocessed)

# Step 3: Train the Naive Bayes model
X_train, X_test, y_train, y_test = train_test_split(X, labels, test_size=0.3, random_state=42)
model = MultinomialNB()
model.fit(X_train, y_train)
```

```
# Step 4: Make predictions and evaluate the model
y_pred = model.predict(X_test)
accuracy = accuracy_score(y_test, y_pred)
print(f"Accuracy: {accuracy}")
print("Classification Report:\n", classification_report(y_test, y_pred))
```

This example uses **TF-IDF** to convert text into numerical features and then trains a **Naive Bayes** model for sentiment classification. You can experiment with different models like **Logistic Regression** or **SVM** for better results.

Step 4: Integrating the Sentiment Analysis Model into Your Chatbot

Once the model is trained, you can integrate it into your chatbot. The model can analyze each user input to determine the sentiment and adjust the chatbot's response accordingly.

Example Integration:

python

```
def chatbot_response(user_input):
    # Preprocess the user input and convert to features
    preprocessed_input = preprocess_text(user_input)
    input_features = vectorizer.transform([' '.join(preprocessed_input)])

    # Predict sentiment
    sentiment = model.predict(input_features)[0]

    # Generate a response based on sentiment
    if sentiment == 'Positive':
```

```
    return "I'm glad to hear that! How can I help you further?"
  elif sentiment == 'Negative':
    return "I'm sorry to hear that! How can I assist you?"
  else:
    return "I see! How can I help you today?"


# Example interaction
user_input = input("You: ")
response = chatbot_response(user_input)
print(f"Bot: {response}")
```

This chatbot response will be influenced by the sentiment of the user input. For example, if the user expresses a negative sentiment, the bot might respond with a more empathetic message.

Use Cases of Sentiment Analysis in Chatbots

Sentiment analysis can be applied to enhance the functionality of chatbots in several ways:

1. **Customer Support**: Sentiment analysis can be used to identify frustrated customers in real-time, allowing the chatbot to escalate the conversation to a human representative when needed.
   - Example: A chatbot identifies a negative sentiment in a customer's query and immediately offers to connect them to a human agent.
2. **Feedback Analysis**: Sentiment analysis allows chatbots to analyze customer feedback, reviews, or surveys to determine overall customer satisfaction and take action accordingly.

- Example: A chatbot can analyze product reviews to classify feedback as positive or negative, and provide insights to businesses.

3. **Personalized Responses**: By detecting the sentiment in a user's message, the chatbot can tailor its responses to be more empathetic or engaging.

   - Example: If the user expresses frustration, the chatbot can respond more empathetically, offering assistance or asking how it can help resolve the issue.

4. **Brand Monitoring**: Sentiment analysis can be applied to social media or online reviews to monitor how people feel about a particular brand or product.

   - Example: A chatbot that monitors brand mentions on social media and can respond or forward negative mentions to customer service.

5. **Market Research**: Sentiment analysis can be used to analyze trends and opinions around certain topics, products, or services, providing valuable insights for businesses.

   - Example: A chatbot analyzes social media data to determine how people feel about an upcoming product launch.

In this chapter, we built a **sentiment analysis chatbot** that can analyze the sentiment of user input and tailor its responses accordingly. We covered the basics of sentiment analysis, walked through building and integrating a sentiment analysis model using machine learning, and explored various **use cases** of sentiment analysis in chatbot applications.

Sentiment analysis can greatly enhance the chatbot experience by making it more intuitive and capable of understanding the emotional tone of user inputs. This allows chatbots to respond more appropriately, improving user satisfaction and engagement.

Chapter 17: Implementing Chatbot Context Management

In this chapter, we will discuss the **importance of context in chatbot conversations**, explore how to manage **multi-turn conversations**, and learn how to **store and use context** effectively with Python. Managing context is a crucial aspect of making chatbots more engaging, natural, and responsive to users' needs.

The Importance of Context in Chatbot Conversations

In human conversation, context plays a vital role in understanding the meaning behind each statement. Without context, a chatbot would treat each user input as isolated, making it difficult to maintain coherent, engaging, and personalized interactions. For example:

- If a user says, "What is the weather like?" and then says, "Will it rain tomorrow?", it's essential for the chatbot to understand that "it" refers to the weather mentioned earlier, not something new.

Context in chatbot conversations allows the bot to:

1. **Maintain continuity** across multiple turns in the conversation.

2. **Understand references** to earlier parts of the conversation, such as locations, names, or previous actions.

3. **Personalize interactions**, making the chatbot capable of remembering user preferences or previous queries.

4. **Disambiguate meaning**—by considering previous inputs, the chatbot can clarify or better understand ambiguous phrases.

Context management helps the chatbot evolve from being a simple question-answering machine to a more interactive and dynamic system capable of sustaining meaningful dialogues.

Managing Multi-Turn Conversations

A **multi-turn conversation** involves several interactions between the user and the chatbot. Each new input from the user builds upon previous exchanges, and the chatbot must maintain an understanding of what has been discussed so far. Multi-turn conversations often require:

- **Tracking User Intent**: The chatbot needs to identify and track the changing intents of the user throughout the conversation.

- **Storing Contextual Information**: The bot must retain important details, such as names, locations, or preferences, that were mentioned earlier.

- **Handling Interruptions**: In a multi-turn conversation, the user might change topics, and the bot needs to adapt to the shift in context.

- **Providing Consistent Responses**: The bot should refer to earlier parts of the conversation when needed, and it should ensure its responses align with previous context.

Challenges in Multi-Turn Conversations

1. **Loss of context**: The chatbot may forget important information from earlier interactions.

2. **Complexity of handling transitions**: Users may switch topics, and the bot needs to identify when the context changes.

3. **Context over multiple sessions**: Ideally, chatbots should remember context even across different user sessions, which adds another layer of complexity.

Storing and Using Context with Python

Context management in chatbots can be implemented in various ways. A simple approach is to store context in memory for a single session (using a dictionary or similar structure). A more sophisticated approach involves storing context in a database or leveraging machine learning models to understand and manage context over longer interactions.

1. Storing Context for a Single Session

We can use a **dictionary** to store context for a single conversation. This method allows the chatbot to retain and access information from previous turns.

Example: Simple Context Management with a Dictionary

python

```
# Initialize context storage (empty dictionary)
context = {}


def update_context(user_input, context):
    # Update context based on user input
    if "name" in user_input.lower():
        context["name"] = user_input.split()[-1]
        return f"Nice to meet you, {context['name']}! How can I assist you today?"

    elif "weather" in user_input.lower():
        location = context.get("location", "the city")
        return f"The weather in {location} is sunny and 75°F."

    elif "location" in user_input.lower():
        location = user_input.split()[-1]
        context["location"] = location
        return f"Got it! I'll remember you're asking about the weather in {location}."

    elif "goodbye" in user_input.lower():
        return f"Goodbye, {context.get('name', 'friend')}! Have a great day."

    else:
```

```python
    return "I'm not sure how to help with that."

# Simulating conversation flow
user_input = input("You: ")
response = update_context(user_input, context)
print(f"Bot: {response}")

user_input = input("You: ")
response = update_context(user_input, context)
print(f"Bot: {response}")
```

Explanation:

- The context dictionary stores user information, such as the **name** and **location**.
- Each time the user provides input, the update_context function modifies the context dictionary based on the user's query.
- The chatbot then responds dynamically, utilizing the stored context to provide more relevant answers.

2. Managing Context Across Sessions

For long-term context management across different sessions, you could use a **database** to store user information, preferences, and past interactions. This enables the chatbot to remember key details, such as the user's name, previous conversations, and preferences, even after the user leaves and comes back.

Example: Storing Context in a Simple Database (SQLite)

python

```python
import sqlite3

# Initialize SQLite database connection
conn = sqlite3.connect('chatbot_context.db')
cursor = conn.cursor()

# Create a table to store user context
cursor.execute('''
CREATE TABLE IF NOT EXISTS user_context (
    user_id TEXT PRIMARY KEY,
    name TEXT,
    location TEXT
)
''')
conn.commit()

def update_context_in_db(user_id, user_input):
    cursor.execute('SELECT * FROM user_context WHERE user_id = ?',
(user_id,))
    user_data = cursor.fetchone()

    if user_data:
        name, location = user_data[1], user_data[2]
    else:
        name, location = None, None

    if "name" in user_input.lower():
        name = user_input.split()[-1]
```

```python
cursor.execute('REPLACE INTO user_context (user_id, name, location)
VALUES (?, ?, ?)', (user_id, name, location))
    conn.commit()
    return f"Nice to meet you, {name}!"


    elif "location" in user_input.lower():
        location = user_input.split()[-1]
        cursor.execute('REPLACE INTO user_context (user_id, name, location)
VALUES (?, ?, ?)', (user_id, name, location))
    conn.commit()
    return f"I've noted your location as {location}."


    elif "weather" in user_input.lower():
        return f"The weather in {location if location else 'your area'} is sunny and
75°F."


    else:
        return "I'm not sure how to assist with that."


# Simulate session with user_id
user_id = "user123"
user_input = input("You: ")
response = update_context_in_db(user_id, user_input)
print(f"Bot: {response}")


user_input = input("You: ")
response = update_context_in_db(user_id, user_input)
print(f"Bot: {response}")
```

Explanation:

- We use **SQLite** to store user context in a database.
- The chatbot retrieves and updates context for a specific user (identified by user_id).
- This allows the chatbot to maintain context over multiple sessions, remembering details like the user's name and location.

3. Using Context with Machine Learning Models

For more sophisticated context management, you can integrate context tracking into your machine learning models. For example, a **Transformer-based model** (like **BERT** or **GPT-3**) can manage conversation context dynamically, allowing the chatbot to understand and generate responses based on the entire conversation history.

Best Practices for Managing Chatbot Context

1. **Use Context Sparingly**: Only store essential information (e.g., user preferences, current session details). Avoid overloading the context, as it can make the chatbot more complex and harder to maintain.
2. **Use Session Expiry**: For temporary context (e.g., a conversation about a specific task), set an expiration time for context. After a certain period or after the task is completed, the context should be cleared.

3. **Contextual Memory**: For better context management, use techniques like **reinforcement learning** or advanced neural network models to track longer-term context across multiple interactions.

4. **Personalization**: Use the stored context to personalize responses, such as greeting the user by name or remembering their preferences.

In this chapter, we explored the **importance of context in chatbot conversations** and discussed how to manage **multi-turn conversations**. We covered several methods for storing and using context:

- Using a dictionary to manage context for a single session.
- Storing and retrieving context from a database for long-term context management.
- Using machine learning models to handle dynamic context in conversations.

Effective context management is essential for creating **engaging, natural, and personalized** chatbot interactions. By maintaining and using context effectively, chatbots can understand users' needs, respond intelligently, and offer a more human-like conversational experience.

Chapter 18: Adding Speech Recognition to Your Chatbot

In this chapter, we will learn how to add **speech recognition** capabilities to a chatbot, allowing users to interact with the bot using voice commands. We will cover how to **integrate speech recognition in Python**, convert **speech to text**, and ultimately build a **voice-enabled chatbot**.

Integrating Speech Recognition in Python

Speech recognition in Python can be easily integrated using various libraries, with **SpeechRecognition** being one of the most popular choices. This library provides simple methods to convert speech into text by interfacing with various speech recognition engines, such as Google Web Speech API, Sphinx, and more.

To get started with speech recognition, we need to install the SpeechRecognition library. Additionally, we will also need a microphone input for capturing voice commands.

Step 1: Installing Required Libraries

bash

```
pip install SpeechRecognition pyttsx3 pyaudio
```

- **SpeechRecognition**: The main library for speech recognition.

- **pyttsx3**: A text-to-speech library for generating speech responses from the chatbot.

- **pyaudio**: Required for capturing microphone input. (If you encounter issues installing pyaudio, you might need to follow platform-specific installation steps.)

Step 2: Importing and Setting Up the SpeechRecognition Library

To begin using speech recognition in Python, you first need to import the speech_recognition module and set up a recognizer instance.

python

```
import speech_recognition as sr

# Initialize recognizer
recognizer = sr.Recognizer()

# Capture audio from the microphone
with sr.Microphone() as source:
    print("Say something...")
    # Adjust for ambient noise levels to ensure accurate recognition
    recognizer.adjust_for_ambient_noise(source)

    # Listen to the user's speech
    audio = recognizer.listen(source)

try:
    # Convert speech to text
```

```
    print("You said: " + recognizer.recognize_google(audio))
  except sr.UnknownValueError:
    print("Sorry, I could not understand the audio")
  except sr.RequestError as e:
    print(f"Could not request results; {e}")
```

Explanation:

- **recognizer.adjust_for_ambient_noise()**: This function ensures that background noise is taken into account when capturing speech, improving recognition accuracy.

- **recognizer.listen()**: This captures the audio from the microphone.

- **recognizer.recognize_google()**: This function sends the captured audio to Google's speech-to-text API to convert it into text.

Converting Speech to Text

The primary goal of integrating speech recognition is to convert **speech to text**. Using the **Google Web Speech API** (via the recognize_google() method) is a simple way to convert speech into text.

However, the SpeechRecognition library also supports other engines such as **Sphinx** (offline), **Microsoft Bing Voice Recognition**, and **IBM Watson** for more advanced or customizable recognition needs.

Here's how to convert speech into text using the **Google Web Speech API**:

python

```
import speech_recognition as sr

# Initialize recognizer
recognizer = sr.Recognizer()

# Capture speech
with sr.Microphone() as source:
    print("Listening...")
    recognizer.adjust_for_ambient_noise(source)
    audio = recognizer.listen(source)

    try:
        # Convert speech to text using Google's API
        text = recognizer.recognize_google(audio)
        print("You said: ", text)
    except sr.UnknownValueError:
        print("Sorry, I didn't understand that.")
    except sr.RequestError:
        print("Sorry, I couldn't connect to the recognition service.")
```

Explanation:

- The recognizer.recognize_google(audio) method sends the audio data to the Google Web Speech API and returns the recognized speech as text.
- If the audio is unclear or the API fails to recognize the speech, it throws an error.

Building a Voice-Enabled Chatbot

Now that we can convert speech to text, we can build a **voice-enabled chatbot** that not only listens to the user but also speaks back to the user. We'll use **pyttsx3** for text-to-speech (TTS) conversion, allowing the chatbot to respond verbally.

Step 1: Importing pyttsx3 for Text-to-Speech

Install the pyttsx3 library if you haven't already.

bash

```
pip install pyttsx3
```

Step 2: Combining Speech Recognition and Text-to-Speech

We will combine **speech recognition** and **text-to-speech** in a chatbot that listens to the user's queries and speaks back responses.

python

```
import speech_recognition as sr
import pyttsx3

# Initialize recognizer and speech engine
recognizer = sr.Recognizer()
engine = pyttsx3.init()

# Function to speak the response
def speak(response):
    engine.say(response)
    engine.runAndWait()
```

```python
# Function to listen and respond
def chatbot_voice_input():
    with sr.Microphone() as source:
        print("Say something...")
        recognizer.adjust_for_ambient_noise(source)
        audio = recognizer.listen(source)

        try:
            user_input = recognizer.recognize_google(audio)
            print("You said:", user_input)

            # Example chatbot responses based on user input
            if "hello" in user_input.lower():
                response = "Hello! How can I assist you today?"
            elif "weather" in user_input.lower():
                response = "The weather is sunny and 75°F."
            elif "bye" in user_input.lower():
                response = "Goodbye! Have a great day."
            else:
                response = "I'm sorry, I didn't understand that."

            speak(response)

        except sr.UnknownValueError:
            print("Sorry, I could not understand your speech.")
            speak("Sorry, I could not understand your speech.")
        except sr.RequestError as e:
            print(f"Error with the speech service: {e}")
            speak(f"Error with the speech service: {e}")
```

Start the voice-enabled chatbot

chatbot_voice_input()

Explanation:

- **pyttsx3** is used to convert the chatbot's text responses into speech.
- **recognizer.recognize_google(audio)** converts the user's speech into text.
- Based on the text input, the bot generates a response and speaks it back to the user using engine.say() and engine.runAndWait().

Enhancing the Voice-Enabled Chatbot

To make the chatbot more interactive and intelligent, we can:

1. **Handle more complex interactions**: Extend the chatbot to handle multiple intents and provide more detailed responses.
2. **Use NLP techniques**: Integrate NLP models like sentiment analysis, intent classification, and named entity recognition to enhance the chatbot's understanding.
3. **Add Context Management**: Use context management to remember user preferences, track conversation history, and handle multi-turn conversations more effectively.

Use Cases of Speech Recognition in Chatbots

Here are some potential use cases of **speech recognition** in chatbots:

1. **Hands-Free Interaction**: Users can interact with chatbots while driving, cooking, or in other situations where typing is not convenient.

2. **Voice-Activated Assistants**: Similar to **Alexa** or **Google Assistant**, voice-enabled chatbots can perform tasks such as setting reminders, providing weather updates, controlling smart home devices, etc.

3. **Customer Support**: Voice recognition can be integrated into customer service bots to allow users to report issues or ask for help by speaking, making it easier for users who prefer voice over text.

4. **Language Learning Apps**: Speech recognition can be used to evaluate pronunciation and fluency, providing feedback to users in real time.

5. **Accessibility**: Speech recognition enables accessibility for users with disabilities, allowing them to interact with systems more easily.

In this chapter, we learned how to integrate **speech recognition** into a chatbot using Python. We explored how to:

- Capture user speech using the SpeechRecognition library.
- Convert speech to text and use it for chatbot interactions.
- Use **pyttsx3** for text-to-speech to make the chatbot respond verbally.

Voice-enabled chatbots enhance the user experience by enabling hands-free interaction and providing a more natural, engaging interface. This integration opens up many possibilities for building more interactive and accessible chatbot applications.

Chapter 19: Using Chatbot Frameworks and Platforms

In this chapter, we will explore some of the **popular chatbot development frameworks** such as **Rasa** and **ChatterBot**, discuss how to **choose the right framework** based on your specific needs, and guide you through the process of **setting up a chatbot using a framework**.

Overview of Popular Chatbot Development Frameworks

Chatbot frameworks provide tools and pre-built functionalities to help developers create intelligent chatbots more efficiently. These frameworks often include NLP modules, intent classification, dialog management, and easy integration with various messaging platforms.

Here, we will focus on two popular frameworks: **Rasa** and **ChatterBot**.

Rasa

Rasa is an open-source conversational AI framework for building chatbots and voice assistants. It provides advanced capabilities for developing machine learning-based chatbots, and is known for its flexibility and customizability. It is designed for building complex conversational workflows and integrates well with external APIs.

Key Features of Rasa:

1. **NLP Integration**: Rasa uses advanced NLP algorithms for intent recognition, entity extraction, and dialog management.
2. **Dialog Management**: Rasa supports conversation flow using stories and rules, allowing you to define complex dialogues.
3. **Customizability**: You can integrate custom actions, API calls, and machine learning models.
4. **Open-source**: Rasa is open-source, providing complete control over your chatbot's functionality.
5. **Integration with Messaging Platforms**: Rasa can be easily integrated with various messaging platforms like Slack, Facebook Messenger, and custom web applications.

Rasa Components:

- **Rasa NLU (Natural Language Understanding)**: Handles intent recognition and entity extraction.
- **Rasa Core**: Manages dialogue and conversation flow based on training data.
- **Rasa X**: A tool to improve Rasa chatbots by collecting real user conversations and training the bot.

How Rasa Works:

1. You define intents and entities in training data (stories).

2. Rasa's NLU component is trained to recognize intents and extract entities.

3. Rasa Core handles conversation flow based on your dialogue policies, and custom actions can be defined for integrations with external services.

ChatterBot

ChatterBot is a Python library designed to help you build conversational chatbots with ease. It provides a simple interface for creating chatbots that can learn from conversations and improve over time.

Key Features of ChatterBot:

1. **Easy to Use**: ChatterBot is beginner-friendly and easy to integrate with Python applications.

2. **Machine Learning-Based**: It uses machine learning algorithms to learn from conversation data and improve its responses.

3. **Language Independent**: ChatterBot supports multiple languages and can be trained on different datasets.

4. **Built-in Training**: It comes with built-in corpus datasets to get started with conversational data quickly.

5. **Customizable**: You can train the chatbot with your own datasets and use custom logic for responses.

How ChatterBot Works:

1. You define a dataset (questions and answers) to train the chatbot.
2. ChatterBot learns from this data and generates responses based on previous conversations.
3. You can customize the logic and add different input-output response patterns for better performance.

Choosing the Right Framework for Your Needs

When deciding which chatbot framework to use, consider the following factors:

1. **Complexity of Your Chatbot**:
   - **Rasa**: Best for building complex, enterprise-grade chatbots that require sophisticated dialogue management, intent recognition, and custom actions.
   - **ChatterBot**: Great for simple chatbots or prototyping, where the focus is on basic conversation and learning from data.
2. **Customization and Extensibility**:

o **Rasa**: Highly customizable and extendable, making it suitable for more advanced use cases where you need to integrate custom actions or third-party APIs.

o **ChatterBot**: Provides a simpler interface and out-of-the-box machine learning capabilities, but it is less flexible compared to Rasa for complex needs.

3. **Integration with External Services**:

o **Rasa**: Rasa supports integrations with external services and databases, which is essential for building chatbots with real-time information and dynamic responses.

o **ChatterBot**: Limited support for external integrations, making it better suited for smaller-scale projects.

4. **Ease of Use**:

o **Rasa**: Steeper learning curve, but the flexibility and control over conversation flow and NLP make it a preferred choice for larger projects.

o **ChatterBot**: Easy to set up and get started with, making it an excellent choice for beginners or rapid prototyping.

5. **Community Support**:

o **Rasa**: Strong community support with extensive documentation, forums, and active contributions from developers.

- ○ **ChatterBot**: Smaller community compared to Rasa, but still offers good documentation and resources for getting started.

Setting Up a Chatbot Using a Framework

Let's walk through the process of setting up a simple chatbot using both **Rasa** and **ChatterBot**.

Setting Up a Rasa Chatbot

Step 1: Install Rasa

First, you need to install **Rasa** using pip:

bash

pip install rasa

Step 2: Initialize a New Rasa Project

Once Rasa is installed, you can initialize a new project:

bash

rasa init --no-prompt

This command creates a new Rasa project with the default directory structure and some sample data.

Step 3: Train Your Rasa Model

Rasa uses training data to learn how to identify intents, entities, and manage dialogue. You can modify the training data in the data/nlu.yml and data/stories.yml files.

After modifying the data, you can train the model:

bash

```
rasa train
```

Step 4: Run Your Rasa Bot

Once the model is trained, you can run your chatbot locally:

bash

```
rasa shell
```

This starts an interactive shell where you can chat with the bot.

Step 5: Custom Actions (Optional)

Rasa also allows you to define **custom actions**, such as calling APIs or interacting with databases. You can define these actions in the actions.py file.

Setting Up a ChatterBot Chatbot

Step 1: Install ChatterBot

You can install **ChatterBot** and its dependencies via pip:

bash

pip install chatterbot chatterbot_corpus

Step 2: Create a Simple ChatterBot Model

You can now create a simple chatbot using ChatterBot. Here's an example:

python

```python
from chatterbot import ChatBot
from chatterbot.trainers import ChatterBotCorpusTrainer

# Create a new chatbot
chatbot = ChatBot('MyBot')

# Set up the trainer
trainer = ChatterBotCorpusTrainer(chatbot)

# Train the chatbot on English corpus data
trainer.train('chatterbot.corpus.english')

# Get a response from the chatbot
response = chatbot.get_response("Hello, how are you?")
print(response)
```

Step 3: Train the Model

ChatterBot uses **corpus data** for training, and you can train the chatbot with predefined datasets. In the example above, we trained the bot using the **English corpus**.

Step 4: Start Interacting with Your Chatbot

You can now interact with the chatbot in a simple loop:

python

```python
while True:
    try:
        user_input = input("You: ")
        response = chatbot.get_response(user_input)
        print(f"Bot: {response}")
    except (KeyboardInterrupt, EOFError, SystemExit):
        break
```

This loop allows the chatbot to continuously respond to user input until interrupted.

In this chapter, we explored popular **chatbot frameworks** like **Rasa** and **ChatterBot**, discussed how to choose the right framework for your needs, and walked through the setup process for both frameworks.

- **Rasa** is ideal for building complex, scalable chatbots with sophisticated dialogue management and NLP capabilities.

- **ChatterBot** is an excellent choice for simple, lightweight chatbots, especially for beginners or prototyping.

Each framework has its strengths, and the choice depends on your project's complexity, required integrations, and level of customization.

Chapter 20: Chatbot Testing and Debugging

In this chapter, we will explore the **best practices for testing chatbots,** how to **identify and fix issues in chatbot conversations,** and introduce some **tools for debugging chatbot code**. As chatbots grow in complexity, thorough testing and debugging are essential to ensure they provide accurate, helpful, and engaging responses to users.

Best Practices for Testing Chatbots

Effective testing ensures that the chatbot can handle a wide range of user inputs, including edge cases and unexpected behavior. Here are some key practices for testing your chatbot:

1. **Unit Testing**: Break down your chatbot into smaller components and test each component individually. For example:
   - Test intent classification to ensure that the bot is recognizing intents correctly.
   - Test response generation to verify that the bot returns the correct response for a given input.
2. **Integration Testing**: Test the entire chatbot flow by simulating multi-turn conversations. This ensures that the bot handles complex dialogues and maintains context throughout the conversation.

3. **Scenario Testing**: Create different scenarios and test how your chatbot responds to them. For instance:

   o **Greetings**: Ensure the chatbot can handle various greetings and respond appropriately.

   o **Fallbacks**: Test how the chatbot handles inputs it doesn't understand.

   o **Interruptions**: Test how the chatbot responds when users interrupt or change topics.

4. **User Simulation**: Simulate real user interactions by typing different queries and testing the bot's responses. This helps identify potential gaps in understanding or handling complex inputs.

5. **Performance Testing**: Measure how well the chatbot performs under heavy load (many simultaneous users). Ensure that it can handle multiple interactions without slowing down or crashing.

6. **A/B Testing**: Conduct A/B testing by running different versions of the chatbot with real users and comparing their interactions. This helps optimize conversation flows and responses.

7. **Cross-Platform Testing**: Test the chatbot on different platforms (e.g., web, mobile, messaging apps) to ensure that it works seamlessly across all devices.

8. **Real-World Testing**: Allow actual users to interact with the chatbot in a production-like environment. This helps identify

issues that may not appear during development or unit testing.

Identifying and Fixing Issues in Chatbot Conversations

As chatbots become more sophisticated, it becomes essential to handle and fix issues efficiently. Here's how to identify common problems in chatbot conversations and resolve them:

1. **Unrecognized Inputs**:
   - **Problem**: The chatbot doesn't understand or misinterprets user input (e.g., "What's the weather like?" → response unrelated to weather).
   - **Solution**: Improve intent classification by providing better training data. Use techniques like **active learning**, where the bot asks for clarification when it doesn't understand a query, and include fallback intents that direct the user to a helpful response (e.g., "I didn't quite understand. Could you please rephrase?").

2. **Context Loss**:
   - **Problem**: The chatbot fails to maintain context in multi-turn conversations (e.g., "Tell me about Paris" → "Where would you like to go?").

o **Solution**: Implement better **context management** to track user inputs and provide responses based on earlier interactions. Use context variables or a session-based memory to store important details like user preferences, names, or previous questions.

3. **Inconsistent Responses**:

   o **Problem**: The chatbot gives inconsistent or incorrect answers (e.g., "What's your name?" → "I am a chatbot" and later "I am called ChatBot").

   o **Solution**: Standardize responses by defining **response templates** for specific intents. Ensure that the bot's responses are consistent, regardless of how users phrase the same question.

4. **Poor Handling of Edge Cases**:

   o **Problem**: The chatbot fails when it encounters unusual or ambiguous queries (e.g., "What is the best pizza?" without specific context).

   o **Solution**: Add additional logic to handle edge cases, including fallback responses, clarifying questions, and predefined responses for common ambiguous queries.

5. **Error Handling**:

   o **Problem**: The chatbot crashes or provides unhelpful responses when it encounters an error (e.g., failing to call an external API).

- o **Solution**: Implement **graceful error handling** by catching exceptions and providing users with friendly error messages. Log errors for debugging purposes, and ensure the chatbot continues to function without breaking.

6. **Long Response Delays**:
   - o **Problem**: The chatbot takes too long to respond, leading to poor user experience.
   - o **Solution**: Optimize backend processes (e.g., API calls, data retrieval) to ensure fast response times. Use **asynchronous programming** to handle multiple tasks simultaneously without blocking the chatbot.

7. **Lack of Personalization**:
   - o **Problem**: The chatbot gives generic responses that don't consider user preferences or context (e.g., not recognizing returning users).
   - o **Solution**: Implement personalization features, such as storing user details (name, preferences) and tailoring responses accordingly. This creates a more engaging and relevant experience.

Tools for Debugging Chatbot Code

Debugging chatbot code can be complex due to the dynamic nature of conversations and the need to manage multiple components (e.g., NLP, dialog flow, integrations). Here are some helpful tools and techniques for debugging chatbots:

1. **Logging and Monitoring**:
   o Use **logging** libraries (e.g., logging in Python) to log important events, responses, and errors in your chatbot. This helps track the flow of conversations and identify where things go wrong.
   o Implement **monitoring tools** to analyze chatbot performance in real-time, including tracking response times, user engagement, and error rates.
2. **Unit Testing Libraries**:
   o Use **unit testing** frameworks like **unittest** or **pytest** in Python to write test cases for individual chatbot components. These libraries allow you to test specific parts of your code (e.g., intent classification, response generation) and ensure they behave as expected.

Example of unit test for a chatbot function:

python

import unittest

```
class TestChatbot(unittest.TestCase):
    def test_weather_intent(self):
        user_input = "What's the weather like today?"
        response = get_response(user_input)  # Assuming get_response is
a function in your chatbot
        self.assertEqual(response, "The weather is sunny and 75°F.")


if __name__ == "__main__":
    unittest.main()
```

3. **Chatbot Testing Platforms**:

   o **Botium**: A testing framework designed for chatbots
       that helps automate conversations, test APIs, and
       integrate with messaging platforms.

   o **TestMyBot**: A chatbot testing tool that allows you to
       test chatbot conversations by defining expected
       intents and responses in test scripts.

   o **Rasa X**: For Rasa-based chatbots, **Rasa X** is an
       excellent tool for testing, debugging, and improving
       chatbot models by collecting real conversations and
       updating training data.

4. **Debugging NLP Models**:

   o For NLP-based chatbots, consider using **interactive
       debuggers** to inspect the behavior of NLP
       components like intent classification and entity
       extraction. You can print intermediate outputs to

check how well the NLP model is interpreting user inputs.

o   For Rasa-based chatbots, use the **Rasa shell** to simulate user inputs and inspect how Rasa interprets intents and entities.

5. **Dialog Management Tools**:

o   Use **dialog flow visualizers** (e.g., Rasa X, Dialogflow) to visualize the conversation flow and understand where things are going wrong in the bot's decision-making process.

o   Analyze **conversation logs** to spot patterns or recurring errors, such as unhandled intents or repeated fallback responses.

6. **Version Control**:

o   Use **Git** for version control to keep track of changes in your chatbot code, configuration files, and training data. This allows you to roll back changes and debug issues related to recent modifications.

7. **Real-Time User Testing**:

o   Deploy your chatbot to a test environment or production and allow real users to interact with it. Gather feedback to identify areas that need improvement, and use logs and metrics to track where users are encountering problems.

In this chapter, we discussed **best practices for testing chatbots**, identified common issues in chatbot conversations, and covered various tools for debugging chatbot code. Effective testing and debugging are critical for ensuring that chatbots perform well and provide a positive user experience.

By following these practices, you can improve the reliability, functionality, and responsiveness of your chatbot, ensuring it meets user expectations and performs efficiently.

Chapter 21: Deploying Your Chatbot

In this chapter, we will explore how to **deploy your chatbot** to make it accessible to users, discuss different hosting options (including cloud platforms like **AWS**, **Google Cloud**, and others), and cover best practices for deploying chatbots across web and mobile interfaces.

Hosting Your Chatbot on Cloud Platforms (AWS, Google Cloud, etc.)

Cloud platforms provide scalable, reliable, and cost-effective hosting solutions for deploying chatbots. The most common cloud platforms for deploying chatbots include **Amazon Web Services (AWS)**, **Google Cloud Platform (GCP)**, and **Microsoft Azure**. These platforms offer a range of services, including compute power, storage, and APIs, making it easier to host and manage your chatbot.

1. Hosting on AWS (Amazon Web Services)

AWS is one of the most widely used cloud platforms for hosting web applications, including chatbots. AWS provides a variety of services that can be used to deploy and manage chatbots, such as **AWS Lambda, Amazon EC2**, and **Amazon Elastic Beanstalk**.

Steps to Deploy a Chatbot on AWS:

1. **Prepare the chatbot code**: Ensure that your chatbot code is ready for deployment. For example, if you're using Python, ensure all dependencies are listed in requirements.txt.

2. **Choose a hosting solution**:

   o **AWS Lambda**: Use AWS Lambda for serverless deployment. Lambda automatically scales and handles requests without requiring you to manage servers.

   o **Amazon EC2**: If you prefer more control over the infrastructure, use EC2 to set up and manage virtual machines to host your chatbot.

   o **Amazon Elastic Beanstalk**: Elastic Beanstalk is a managed service that simplifies the deployment process by automatically handling scaling, load balancing, and monitoring.

Example: Deploying with AWS Lambda:

1. Package your chatbot into a serverless function using AWS Lambda.

2. Create an API using **Amazon API Gateway** to expose the Lambda function to the web.

3. Set up an **IAM Role** to allow API Gateway to invoke the Lambda function.

4. Deploy and test your chatbot.

2. Hosting on Google Cloud (GCP)

Google Cloud Platform (GCP) provides services like **Google App Engine (GAE)**, **Google Kubernetes Engine (GKE)**, and **Google Cloud Functions** for deploying chatbots.

Steps to Deploy a Chatbot on GCP:

1. **Prepare the chatbot code**: Ensure all dependencies are ready for deployment, similar to AWS.
2. **Choose a hosting solution**:
   - **Google Cloud Functions**: If you want a serverless architecture, use Cloud Functions. These functions are executed in response to HTTP requests.
   - **Google Kubernetes Engine (GKE)**: Use GKE if you want to deploy your chatbot in containers and need more control over orchestration.
   - **Google App Engine (GAE)**: For a simpler solution, you can use GAE to deploy your chatbot as a web application without worrying about infrastructure management.

Example: Deploying with Google Cloud Functions:

1. Write your chatbot code as a Python function.
2. Use the **Google Cloud SDK** to deploy the function to Google Cloud.

3. Create an **HTTP trigger** to expose the function via a web endpoint.

4. Test and verify the chatbot is working correctly.

3. Hosting on Microsoft Azure

Azure provides a variety of services for deploying chatbots, including **Azure Functions** (serverless), **Azure App Service** (PaaS), and **Azure Kubernetes Service** (AKS).

Steps to Deploy a Chatbot on Azure:

1. **Prepare your chatbot code**.

2. **Choose a hosting service**: You can use **Azure App Service** for simple web app deployment or **Azure Functions** for a serverless deployment.

3. **Set up API endpoints** using **Azure API Management** to expose the chatbot for web access.

4. **Deploy and scale**: Use Azure's scaling options to handle increased traffic.

Making Your Chatbot Accessible Through Web and Mobile Interfaces

After deploying your chatbot to the cloud, the next step is to make it accessible to users through web and mobile interfaces. You can achieve this by integrating the chatbot with various front-end technologies.

1. Web Interface for Chatbot

To make your chatbot accessible through a web interface, you can integrate it into a website using **JavaScript** or **HTML**. One of the most common ways to add a chatbot to a website is by using a **web-based chat interface** that interacts with the backend via APIs (RESTful or WebSockets).

Example: Integrating a Web Chat Interface:

1. **Frontend (HTML/JS)**: Use a simple web interface with an input field and chat window.
2. **Backend (API)**: Use the cloud-hosted chatbot API (e.g., AWS Lambda or GCP Cloud Function) to handle user queries.
3. **WebSocket or REST API**: Use WebSocket for real-time communication or REST API for standard request-response interactions.

Example: Using JavaScript and WebSockets for Web Integration:

html

```
<!DOCTYPE html>
<html lang="en">
```

```html
<head>
  <meta charset="UTF-8">
  <meta name="viewport" content="width=device-width, initial-scale=1.0">
  <title>Chatbot</title>
</head>
<body>
  <div id="chatbox"></div>
  <input type="text" id="user_input" placeholder="Type a message">
  <button onclick="sendMessage()">Send</button>

  <script>
    const ws = new WebSocket('wss://your-chatbot-endpoint.com');  // WebSocket URL for your chatbot API

    function sendMessage() {
      const message = document.getElementById('user_input').value;
      ws.send(JSON.stringify({ message }));
    }

    ws.onmessage = function(event) {
      const response = JSON.parse(event.data);
      document.getElementById('chatbox').innerText += "Bot: " + response.message + "\n";
    };
  </script>
</body>
</html>
```

In this example, a user sends a message through an input field, and the chatbot responds via WebSockets.

2. Mobile Interface for Chatbot

To make the chatbot available on mobile devices, you can integrate it with mobile applications. This can be done using native mobile SDKs or by embedding the chatbot into a mobile app via a **webview** or **native components**.

- **Native SDKs**: Use mobile SDKs like **Facebook Messenger SDK**, **WhatsApp Business API**, or **Twilio** to integrate chatbots into messaging platforms.
- **WebView**: Embed a web-based chatbot interface within a mobile app using a WebView (for both Android and iOS).
- **Mobile APIs**: Expose your chatbot via APIs, allowing mobile apps to send and receive messages.

Example: Using WebView in Android for Chatbot Integration:

java

```
WebView webView = findViewById(R.id.webview);
webView.getSettings().setJavaScriptEnabled(true);
webView.loadUrl("https://your-chatbot-web-interface.com");
```

Example: Using Twilio API for SMS Integration:

1. Set up a **Twilio account** to send and receive SMS messages.
2. Use Twilio's **Programmable Messaging API** to connect your chatbot with SMS.

Best Practices for Deployment

When deploying a chatbot, it's important to follow **best practices** to ensure reliability, scalability, and a positive user experience. Here are some key practices to keep in mind:

1. **Scalability**: Ensure your chatbot can scale based on traffic. Use auto-scaling features of cloud platforms (e.g., **AWS Lambda**, **Google Cloud Functions**) to handle fluctuations in traffic.

2. **Security**: Implement security best practices to protect user data. Use **SSL/TLS encryption** for web and mobile interfaces, and ensure that APIs are properly secured (e.g., using API keys or OAuth).

3. **Logging and Monitoring**: Set up logging to capture errors, user interactions, and performance data. Use **cloud monitoring tools** like **AWS CloudWatch**, **Google Stackdriver**, or **Azure Monitor** to track the health of your chatbot and troubleshoot issues in real-time.

4. **Backup and Redundancy**: Ensure your deployment is fault-tolerant. Use backups for data and redundancy for critical components, especially in production environments.

5. **Continuous Integration/Continuous Deployment (CI/CD)**: Set up a CI/CD pipeline to automate the process of deploying updates and new features to your chatbot. Use tools like **GitLab CI**, **Jenkins**, or **AWS CodePipeline** for continuous integration and deployment.

6. **User Testing**: Before deploying to a wide audience, conduct thorough user testing in a staging environment to identify and fix issues that could affect user experience.

7. **Optimization**: Optimize your chatbot's response times by caching frequently used data and reducing the overhead of third-party API calls.

8. **Compliance**: Ensure that your chatbot complies with relevant regulations, such as **GDPR** for European users, and that it handles sensitive data securely.

In this chapter, we explored the process of deploying your chatbot to the cloud, making it accessible through **web and mobile interfaces**, and following **best practices for deployment**. By hosting your chatbot on platforms like AWS, Google Cloud, or Microsoft Azure, you can ensure scalability and reliability. Integrating with web and mobile interfaces allows users to interact with your chatbot seamlessly.

Following deployment best practices will help you ensure a smooth user experience, secure your chatbot, and optimize performance for a larger audience.

Chapter 22: Enhancing Chatbot User Experience

In this chapter, we will explore how to **enhance the user experience (UX)** of your chatbot by focusing on **usability and engagement**, incorporating **rich media** (images, buttons, etc.) into responses, and applying **UX design principles** specifically tailored to chatbot interactions. A well-designed chatbot can significantly improve user satisfaction, making interactions more intuitive, engaging, and effective.

Designing for Usability and Engagement

When designing a chatbot, **usability** and **engagement** are two key factors that determine how effectively the chatbot serves users. A user-friendly chatbot ensures that users can easily navigate interactions and accomplish their tasks, while an engaging chatbot keeps users interested and encourages continued interaction.

1. Usability in Chatbot Design

Usability refers to how easily users can interact with the chatbot and achieve their goals. A usable chatbot should:

- **Have clear instructions**: Users should know what they can do with the chatbot and how to interact with it.
- **Provide quick responses**: Delays in responses can frustrate users, so aim for fast and efficient replies.

- **Offer simple interactions**: Avoid making users type long sentences. Simplify interactions by guiding them through the process.
- **Be easy to restart**: If a conversation goes off track, provide an easy way to restart or redirect the user.
- **Be transparent**: Let users know what the chatbot can and cannot do, and set expectations clearly.

Example of Usability Best Practices:

- Use **short, clear language** that's easy for users to understand.
- Ensure that the chatbot provides options when it doesn't understand the user (e.g., "Can you rephrase your question?").
- Allow users to get back to the main menu or restart the conversation at any time with a simple command (e.g., "Restart" or "Main Menu").

2. Engagement in Chatbot Design

Engagement focuses on making the conversation enjoyable, interactive, and personal. An engaging chatbot encourages users to continue interacting by:

- **Personalizing the experience**: Refer to the user by name and remember their preferences or past interactions.

- **Being conversational**: Use friendly, informal language to create a conversational tone.

- **Offering valuable interactions**: Provide information or services that are genuinely helpful and relevant to the user's needs.

- **Being interactive**: Encourage user participation by using options, buttons, and interactive elements.

Example of Engagement Best Practices:

- Use **personalized greetings** (e.g., "Hello, John! How can I assist you today?").

- Use **dynamic responses** that change based on user input (e.g., offering different responses depending on the user's query).

- Use **emotion or tone** to keep the conversation lively (e.g., "I'm sorry to hear that" for negative sentiments).

Adding Rich Media (Images, Buttons, etc.) to Chatbot Responses
Adding **rich media** such as images, videos, buttons, quick replies, and carousels can greatly enhance the user experience by making conversations more dynamic, visually appealing, and interactive.

1. Images and Videos

Visual content like images and videos can help users better understand the information provided by the chatbot and create a more immersive experience.

- **Use Images**: If your chatbot is providing information about a product or service, displaying an image can enhance clarity and engage users. For instance, when a user asks about a product, the chatbot can display an image of the product.
- **Use Videos**: If you need to explain a process or feature, a short tutorial video can be very helpful.

Example:

python

```
response = {
    "text": "Here's a picture of the product you asked about:",
    "image": "https://example.com/product.jpg"
}
```

2. Buttons and Quick Replies

Interactive elements like **buttons** and **quick replies** allow users to choose from a set of predefined options rather than typing out responses. This reduces friction and speeds up the conversation. Buttons can guide users through the chatbot, and quick replies can be used for common responses.

- **Buttons**: Can be used to offer choices, such as selecting an option or navigating between different sections of the chatbot.

- **Quick Replies**: Allow users to tap on suggested replies or actions, speeding up the interaction.

Example:

python

```
response = {
    "text": "What would you like to do?",
    "buttons": [
        {"title": "Check weather", "payload": "weather"},
        {"title": "Order food", "payload": "order_food"},
        {"title": "Help", "payload": "help"}
    ]
}
```

3. Carousels

A **carousel** is a component that displays multiple items (such as product images or service options) in a horizontally scrollable manner. This is ideal for presenting a list of items, such as product recommendations, news articles, or services.

Example:

python

```
response = {
```

```
  "text": "Here are some products you might like:",
  "carousel": [
      {"image_url": "https://example.com/product1.jpg", "title": "Product 1",
"payload": "product1_details"},
      {"image_url": "https://example.com/product2.jpg", "title": "Product 2",
"payload": "product2_details"}
  ]
}
```

4. Interactive Cards

Interactive cards are a combination of buttons, images, and text that appear as a complete UI element. They are often used for more complex interactions, such as surveys, appointment scheduling, or event booking.

User Experience (UX) Design for Chatbots

The ultimate goal of UX design for chatbots is to make the interaction as intuitive, efficient, and satisfying as possible. Here are key UX design principles specifically tailored for chatbots:

1. Understand User Intent

Ensure that the chatbot can accurately identify and understand user intent. Use intent recognition models to classify what users want to do (e.g., asking for the weather, making a reservation, or getting product recommendations).

- **Clarity**: The chatbot should be able to ask for clarification if it doesn't understand a user's intent, avoiding frustration.
- **Error Handling**: When the chatbot can't understand something, provide helpful prompts like "Can you clarify your request?" or "I'm sorry, I didn't catch that."

2. Keep the Conversation Flow Natural

- **Conversational Flow**: Ensure that the conversation feels natural and smooth. Avoid rigid scripts and provide room for flexibility.
- **Contextual Awareness**: Maintain context over multiple interactions. If the user asks for weather details and then inquires about a specific city, the chatbot should remember that context.
- **Feedback Loops**: When users provide input, ensure the bot acknowledges the request and responds in a meaningful way.

3. Minimalist Design and Clear Navigation

In chatbot design, simplicity is key. Don't overwhelm the user with too many options or information. Offer clear choices and intuitive navigation paths.

- **Limit User Choices**: Present users with 3–5 options at a time to avoid decision fatigue.

- **Progressive Disclosure**: Show information progressively rather than all at once. This keeps users focused on the current task and prevents overwhelming them.

4. Ensure Responsiveness

The chatbot should respond quickly and consistently. Slow response times can lead to frustration and disengagement. Additionally, ensure the bot's responses are appropriate for mobile devices, where interactions tend to be shorter and faster.

5. Use Personalization

Personalize the conversation by remembering user preferences, using their name, and tailoring responses based on past interactions. A personalized experience builds a deeper connection with the user and increases engagement.

- **User Profiles**: If possible, maintain a simple user profile to provide tailored recommendations, reminders, and responses.
- **Custom Greetings**: Use the user's name in greetings or responses to create a more personal experience.

6. Test with Real Users

The best way to ensure your chatbot delivers an optimal UX is by conducting usability testing with real users. Observe how they interact with the bot, gather feedback, and refine the chatbot based on their suggestions. Testing with diverse users helps identify pain points and areas for improvement.

In this chapter, we explored how to **enhance chatbot user experience** by focusing on usability, engagement, and UX design principles. We discussed how to:

- Design chatbot interactions that are user-friendly and engaging.
- Use **rich media** (images, buttons, carousels) to make conversations more dynamic and visually appealing.
- Apply **UX design principles** to ensure a smooth and natural conversation flow.
- Use personalization and error-handling strategies to improve the chatbot's effectiveness.

By following these best practices, you can build chatbots that offer a delightful and engaging experience for users, leading to higher user satisfaction and retention.

Chapter 23: Security and Privacy in Chatbot Development

In this chapter, we will explore the critical aspects of **security** and **privacy** in chatbot development. As chatbots become more integrated into everyday life, they handle sensitive user information, making it crucial to ensure that they are secure and protect users' privacy. We will discuss how to **ensure user data privacy, prevent common security issues**, and follow **best practices** to secure chatbot applications.

Ensuring User Data Privacy in Chatbot Conversations

User privacy is one of the most important considerations in chatbot development. Chatbots often process sensitive information, such as personal data, account credentials, or even payment information. Therefore, it is crucial to adopt measures that ensure user data is handled with care and protected against unauthorized access.

1. Data Encryption

Encryption is one of the fundamental security measures to protect data in transit and at rest. By encrypting data, you make it unreadable to unauthorized users or systems.

- **Encryption in Transit**: Use **SSL/TLS** (Secure Socket Layer/Transport Layer Security) to encrypt data while it travels between the chatbot and the user. This ensures that any communication over the web is secure.

- o Example: Ensure that your chatbot's web interface is hosted on https://, indicating that SSL is in use.
- **Encryption at Rest**: If your chatbot stores sensitive data in a database, it should be encrypted while at rest.
  - o Example: Use **AES-256** (Advanced Encryption Standard) to encrypt sensitive user data before storing it.

2. Anonymization and Pseudonymization

In some cases, you may not need to store personally identifiable information (PII). If you do need to collect data, you can implement **anonymization** or **pseudonymization** techniques to obscure sensitive information.

- **Anonymization**: The process of removing any information that can identify the user directly. This way, even if data is breached, it cannot be traced back to the individual.
  - o Example: Replacing a user's name with a random identifier or using only their IP address without associating it with personal data.
- **Pseudonymization**: The process of replacing personal identifiers with pseudonyms or placeholders, allowing the information to be traced back to the individual only under specific circumstances.

- o Example: Replacing a user's email address with a pseudonym, but keeping the real email address in a separate secure database.

3. Limiting Data Collection

Collect only the data that is necessary for the chatbot to function. Avoid requesting excessive information from users that might compromise their privacy.

- **Minimal Data Collection**: Gather only the minimum amount of data required to fulfill the user's request. For example, if the user is asking for the weather, you do not need their location history.
- **Clear Consent**: Always ask users for explicit consent before collecting any data. Use clear language to explain what data will be collected and how it will be used.

Example:

python

```
def ask_for_consent():
    user_input = input("To proceed, we need your consent to collect your location
for weather updates. Do you consent? (yes/no): ")
    if user_input.lower() == "yes":
        return True
    else:
        return False
```

4. Implementing User Control and Access Management

Give users control over their data by allowing them to:

- **View** what information the chatbot has collected about them.
- **Delete** or modify personal information.
- **Withdraw consent** for data collection at any time.

Example: Offer a command like "Delete my data" or "Update my preferences" so users can manage their data easily.

5. User Authentication

For chatbots that handle sensitive information (e.g., banking, e-commerce), implement **user authentication** to ensure that only authorized users can access specific services. You can use authentication methods such as:

- **Two-Factor Authentication (2FA)**: Requires the user to provide two forms of identification (e.g., a password and a verification code sent to their phone).
- **OAuth**: A standard for token-based authentication, which allows users to log in via third-party services like Google or Facebook, without sharing their password with the chatbot.

Preventing Common Security Issues in Chatbots

There are several **common security vulnerabilities** that chatbots are prone to. Here are some key security issues and how to prevent them:

1. Injection Attacks

Chatbots that interact with databases or external systems are vulnerable to injection attacks, such as **SQL injection** or **Command injection**.

- **SQL Injection**: An attacker might inject malicious SQL code into user inputs that are passed to the database, causing unauthorized data access or manipulation.
    - **Prevention**: Use **prepared statements** or **parameterized queries** to avoid direct SQL injection.
    - Example (using Python and SQLite):

      python

      ```
      cursor.execute("SELECT * FROM users WHERE username = ?", (username,))
      ```

- **Command Injection**: An attacker might inject malicious commands that can be executed on the server.
    - **Prevention**: Always validate and sanitize user input before passing it to system-level commands.

2. Cross-Site Scripting (XSS)

Cross-Site Scripting (XSS) attacks occur when a chatbot allows users to input HTML or JavaScript that is then rendered in the browser, allowing attackers to inject malicious scripts.

- **Prevention**: Use **output encoding** or **escaping** to prevent user inputs from being executed as code. Additionally, use security headers like **Content Security Policy (CSP)** to restrict the types of scripts that can be executed.

3. Data Breach Vulnerabilities

Chatbots that store user data must be protected against data breaches, which can expose sensitive information.

- **Prevention**: Regularly audit and update security protocols. Use firewalls, encryption, and access controls to prevent unauthorized access. Also, ensure that user data is stored in **secure databases**.

4. Phishing and Social Engineering Attacks

Phishing and social engineering attacks involve manipulating users to divulge sensitive information. Attackers may attempt to impersonate the chatbot and trick users into revealing credentials or personal data.

- **Prevention**: Implement **authentication mechanisms** and always validate user identity before processing sensitive requests. Ensure that the chatbot does not ask for sensitive information like passwords or credit card details unless absolutely necessary.

Best Practices for Securing Chatbot Applications

Here are some **best practices** for securing chatbot applications:

1. Secure API Integrations

If your chatbot integrates with third-party APIs (e.g., for payment processing, social media integration, etc.), ensure that the API endpoints are secure. Use **HTTPS** for all communication with external APIs and **API keys** to authenticate requests.

2. Regular Security Audits

Conduct regular security audits and vulnerability scans to identify potential weaknesses in the chatbot system. Tools like **OWASP ZAP** or **Burp Suite** can help perform automated security testing on your chatbot's APIs and endpoints.

3. Secure the Bot's Infrastructure

Ensure that the chatbot's hosting environment is secure. If using cloud services (e.g., AWS, GCP, or Azure), take advantage of their security features, such as **IAM roles**, **firewalls**, and **VPCs** to isolate your chatbot's resources and restrict access.

4. Logging and Monitoring

Set up logging to capture critical events and security-related activities (e.g., unauthorized access attempts, data modification). Use monitoring tools to keep track of your chatbot's performance and security, and set up alerts for suspicious behavior.

5. Handle Sensitive Data Carefully

Avoid storing sensitive data like passwords, credit card details, or social security numbers. If storing such data is necessary, encrypt it using industry-standard encryption methods. Do not store plain text passwords, and always use **hashed and salted** passwords.

In this chapter, we covered the importance of **security** and **privacy** in chatbot development. By implementing strong security measures such as **data encryption, user authentication**, and **secure API integrations**, you can protect both your chatbot and users from potential threats.

Additionally, by following best practices for handling sensitive data, preventing common security vulnerabilities, and conducting regular audits, you can ensure that your chatbot operates securely and in compliance with privacy regulations.

By following these guidelines, you can build a secure, reliable, and trustworthy chatbot that keeps user data safe while providing a high-quality user experience.

Chapter 24: The Future of Chatbots and NLP

In this chapter, we will explore the **emerging trends** in chatbot technology, examine the role of **AI** and **NLP** in shaping the future of conversational bots, and share **final thoughts** on how to build innovative, smart chatbots that meet the growing needs of users and businesses.

Emerging Trends in Chatbot Technology

Chatbots and Natural Language Processing (NLP) are rapidly evolving technologies. Here are some of the **key trends** that will shape the future of chatbot development:

1. Conversational AI with Deep Learning

Deep learning models, especially **transformers** (like **BERT**, **GPT-3**, and **T5**), are revolutionizing chatbot capabilities. These models excel at understanding and generating human-like text, enabling more advanced conversational AI systems.

- **GPT-3** and similar models are pushing the boundaries of language generation, allowing chatbots to engage in more natural, dynamic conversations that are contextually aware and highly engaging.
- Future chatbots powered by deep learning models will have improved understanding, greater conversational depth, and

the ability to handle multi-turn conversations with more context awareness.

2. Multimodal Chatbots

While text-based chatbots are widely used, the future of conversational bots is likely to include **multimodal** capabilities, where chatbots will not only understand text but also images, audio, and video. For example, a chatbot could:

- Recognize an image and describe its contents (e.g., "This is a picture of a cat").
- Use **voice input** and **output** to allow users to interact more seamlessly.
- Combine text, images, and video to create richer, more engaging experiences.

With multimodal capabilities, chatbots will become more versatile and adaptable to different types of user inputs.

3. Personalization and Emotional Intelligence

Personalized chatbots that understand user preferences and emotions will become a key feature. Using **sentiment analysis**, **emotion recognition**, and **user profiling**, future chatbots will be able to:

- Respond empathetically to users based on the emotional tone of their messages (e.g., offering sympathy to a frustrated user or congratulating them for an achievement).
- Adapt conversations to match individual user preferences, such as their preferred language, style of communication, or type of service.

This level of personalization will create a deeper connection between users and chatbots, leading to more meaningful and effective interactions.

4. Integration with IoT (Internet of Things)

As the **Internet of Things (IoT)** continues to grow, chatbots will become a key interface for controlling smart devices. Future chatbots will be able to:

- Interact with a wide range of connected devices (e.g., smart lights, thermostats, wearables) through conversational interfaces.
- Provide real-time updates and notifications from IoT devices, allowing users to control their smart environments through simple voice or text commands.

The integration of chatbots with IoT systems will create seamless, hands-free experiences for users to manage their homes, health, and other connected devices.

5. Autonomous Chatbots with Machine Learning

As machine learning continues to evolve, chatbots will be able to **learn autonomously** from user interactions. This means that, rather than relying solely on predefined rules, chatbots will:

- Continuously improve their performance by learning from real-time conversations.
- Adjust their responses based on the context, preferences, and behaviors of users, becoming more efficient and effective over time.

Autonomous learning will lead to chatbots that become more accurate and better at handling complex interactions, without requiring frequent manual updates.

6. Conversational Commerce (C-Commerce)

The rise of **conversational commerce** is a significant trend. Chatbots will increasingly be used to facilitate shopping and transactions directly through conversations. With the ability to recommend products, handle payments, and track orders, chatbots will become the primary interface for e-commerce.

- Chatbots will guide users through the entire purchase process, from browsing products to completing checkout, all within the conversational interface.
- This will make online shopping more seamless, efficient, and personalized.

The Role of AI and NLP in the Future of Conversational Bots

As chatbot technology matures, **AI** and **NLP** will continue to play a central role in shaping the future of conversational bots. Here's how these technologies will evolve:

1. Advancements in NLP Models

NLP models will continue to improve in terms of accuracy, efficiency, and complexity. Key advancements will include:

- **Better contextual understanding**: Future NLP models will understand the meaning behind words in the context of entire conversations, reducing the occurrence of misunderstandings.
- **Multilingual support**: NLP models will become more proficient in understanding and generating multiple languages, enabling truly global chatbots that can cater to users in different regions.

2. Natural, Human-Like Conversations

The goal of conversational AI is to replicate human-like interactions. With **deep learning** and **advanced NLP models**, chatbots will evolve to understand not only the meaning of words but also nuances such as:

- **Sarcasm**: Detecting when a user is being sarcastic and adjusting responses accordingly.

- **Ambiguity**: Clarifying vague or ambiguous statements by asking clarifying questions.

- **Intent and emotion**: Recognizing user intent and emotions in real-time to adapt responses to fit the conversation flow.

3. AI-Powered Recommendations

AI will enable chatbots to make highly personalized recommendations based on user behavior and historical data. For instance:

- Chatbots will suggest products, services, or content that align with a user's preferences, browsing history, and previous interactions.

- AI models will be able to predict future user needs and offer proactive assistance, making chatbots more helpful and predictive.

4. Ethical AI and Bias Mitigation

As AI becomes more integrated into our lives, ethical concerns around fairness, transparency, and bias in AI models will continue to grow. The future of chatbot development will involve efforts to:

- **Minimize bias** in training data to prevent discriminatory behavior from chatbots.

- Implement **transparent AI** practices that allow users to understand how decisions are made and how their data is used.
- Establish clear guidelines for **ethical chatbot design** to ensure that chatbots act responsibly and align with societal values.

Final Thoughts on Building Innovative, Smart Chatbots

Building innovative, smart chatbots requires a combination of the right technology, design principles, and continuous iteration. Here are some final thoughts for creating successful chatbots:

1. Focus on User-Centered Design

The user should always be at the center of the chatbot design process. Ensure that your chatbot's functionality and conversation flow align with user needs and expectations. Keep the conversation simple, intuitive, and human-like, while focusing on solving real-world problems.

2. Continuous Learning and Improvement

Chatbot development is an ongoing process. As new interactions occur, chatbots should continuously learn and improve. Leverage **machine learning** and **user feedback** to enhance chatbot performance and make them smarter over time.

3. Embrace Multimodal Interactions

Don't limit your chatbot to text-based communication. Explore opportunities to make it multimodal—integrating voice, images, videos, and even augmented reality (AR) to enhance user experience and engagement.

4. Prioritize Security and Privacy

As chatbots handle more personal and sensitive data, **security** and **privacy** will be paramount. Implement strong encryption, secure authentication, and clear privacy policies to protect user data and build trust.

5. Stay Updated with Emerging Technologies

The field of chatbot development is rapidly evolving. Stay informed about the latest advancements in **AI**, **NLP**, and **machine learning** to ensure your chatbot remains competitive and innovative.

6. Strive for Meaningful Interactions

The future of chatbots is not just about automating simple tasks but about creating meaningful, human-like interactions. Focus on providing value to users through personalized responses, efficient problem-solving, and proactive assistance.

In this chapter, we discussed the **future of chatbots and NLP**, highlighting emerging trends such as deep learning, multimodal interactions, conversational commerce, and AI-powered recommendations. We also explored how **AI** and **NLP** will shape the evolution of conversational bots, enabling smarter, more personalized interactions.

Finally, we shared best practices for building innovative, user-friendly chatbots that prioritize **user-centered design**, **continuous learning**, **security**, and **privacy**. By embracing these principles, you can create chatbots that not only meet user expectations but also pave the way for the future of conversational AI.

www.ingramcontent.com/pod-product-compliance
Lightning Source LLC
La Vergne TN
LVHW022341060326
832902LV00022B/4166